# THE ABC's OF SITE SELECTION

# THE ABC'S OF SITE SELECTION

## SELECTION

How to Pick Winners and Avoid Losers

Frank Raeon

"I thought it was a great LOCATION"

**To order additional copies of this book, contact:**
Xlibris LLC
1-888-795-4274
www.Xlibris.com
Orders@Xlibris.com
83259

# CONTENTS

Preface .................................................................................. 11
Introduction ......................................................................... 15

**Chapter One**
The Six Keys To Making "Smart" Site Selection Decisions ......................... 19

**Chapter Two**
Primary Site Selection Factors .................................................. 28

**Chapter Three**
Secondary Site Selection Factors ............................................... 45

**Chapter Four**
Selecting The Type of Location Which Best Suits Your Business .............. 60

**Chapter Five**
Other Important Site Selection Influences and Related Factors ............ 79

**Chapter Six**
Estimating Retail and Restaurant Sales ....................................... 121

**Chapter Seven**
Creating A Site Selection Scorecard .......................................... 125

**Chapter Eight**
The Importance of Demographics and Psychographics ..................... 135

**Chapter Nine**
Short and Long Form Customer Surveys ...................................... 142

**Chapter Ten**
Location, Location, Location ..................................................... 149

Conclusion ....................................................................... 159
About the Author .............................................................. 163
Book Audience ................................................................. 165
Index ............................................................................... 167

# DEDICATION

This self help guidebook is dedicated to the seemingly endless legions of people who either have a strong desire to go into business for themselves, or, already operate one or more small businesses. They are the real entrepreneurs—the people who have a dream to be their own boss and a drive to succeed in spite of the many obstacles and risks which they will encounter.

# PREFACE

The idea for this guidebook originated many years ago. Going back to the Alibi, the mom-and-pop restaurant which my parents operated, I have always been intrigued with why businesses either succeeded or failed at their respective locations.

Before becoming involved in commercial real estate I had the good fortune to work as a City Planning and Development Director at the municipal level. This provided me with the opportunity to ask anyone and everyone who came into my office what was it that made them decide on a particular location?

As a result of working with national retail and restaurant companies, I learned that making location decisions always originated with a set of site selection criteria—something which I have observed over many years is little-known to almost every start-up businessperson as well as to many of the businesspeople who operate one or perhaps only a small number of retail stores or restaurants. In addition to being either in or very near "the action," I have found that cheap rent, vacant space, a sense of urgency, and proximity to home are major influences that many small businesspeople cite when explaining how they go about making location decisions.

After establishing a working relationship with McDonald's real estate representatives, I was taught to never bring them a site which I would not personally invest my own money in. Ever since then this has been the "gold" standard that I have used to guide me. in making site selection recommendations.

In the future, businesses will continue to open and close. This is one prediction that is extremely easy to make. It is also a statement that no one ever disagrees with because it is factual as opposed to being based upon opinion. The hope of this guidebook and the inspiration for the information which follows is to be able to help decision makers minimize mistakes and maximize opportunities.

We live in an impatient world, one where getting things instantly has become the new mind-set. Quick and fast are well established buzzwords. However, when it comes to making "smart" location decisions nothing could be further from the truth! The sooner you understand that site selection is a process, one which requires hours and hours of making site visits and analysis, the better off both you and your pocketbook will be.

My primary goal in writing this guidebook is to educate you about site selection; what you learn will better position you to succeed. Another of my goals is to help you become more financially secure. These are both achievable if you are willing to dedicate yourself to employing a systematic approach to site selection.

I hope you understand that disappointment, disillusionment, and failure are preventable. However, to insure that none of these negative consequences come to dominate your future vocabulary you will always need to do your homework. You need to build a strong foundation. Giving you the tools to make "smart" location decisions is what this guidebook is all about. If you ignore my advice, especially what I refer to as The Six Keys, you may end up having either a short and unproductive business career, or, you may never achieve the store or restaurant expansion that you once envisioned.

The inspiration for this guidebook comes from three sources: the authors of various site selection books which I have read over many years, the companies who I have helped find "home run" locations during the past twenty-five years, and the large number of entrepreneurs I have talked with and periodically assisted.

The former group indirectly acted as my early mentors and provided me with a strong and continuing interest in learning more about site selection and location decision analysis—something which I expect will continue to interest me for the rest of my life.

The second group taught me that a systematic approach was essential to making "smart" location decisions. These were people who left no stone unturned in completing their field work and their research. They are the people who understood exactly which sites had the potential to become "home run" locations.

As for the latter group, I quickly observed that the great majority had very little understanding of site selection. These were people who were much more likely to make independent decisions rather than rely on the advice and expertise of one or more professionals. Thus, I realized there was a need for the types of services which I pride myself on providing. In the end, these are the people who prompted me to form my consulting company—*Location Decision Advisors*.

To each and all of these groups I am deeply indebted and very thankful.

# INTRODUCTION

This guidebook is directed at each and every person who is involved in making retail and restaurant site selection decisions. Anyone who owns a small business, is interested in starting their own business, or advises people on buying or leasing commercial real estate should become familiar with not only its terms, but with the methodology which it identifies for selecting profitable locations.

Over a long period of time I have learned that for many small businesspeople site selection is more about emotion, convenience, and cheap rent than it is about working with a commercial realtor or real estate consultant and employing a systematic and disciplined decision-making approach. Indeed, this simplistic rationale helps explain why so many small businesses fail within a relatively short period of time.

**Site selection is neither an art nor a science**. Rather, it is a combination of both. It is a process which involves doing a significant amount of homework—something which a few people are willing to invest a lot of time doing while most others are only interested in spending a little time on. In the long run, doing your homework is the only way to justify making what can turn out to be a very significant monetary investment.

This guidebook is intended to be comprehensive in scope while being basic in its description of terms. It is meant to give you, the small businessperson as well as the person who is contemplating opening a new business, the insights which are required to make "smart" location as well as "smart" site selection decisions. Indeed, if you understand and employ the terms which I have identified you will greatly increase the likelihood of being able to select one or more "home run" locations.

The small size of this guidebook is intentional. It has been designed to be kept in a briefcase, a purse, or even the glove compartment box of the vehicle you drive rather than on some book shelf or desk top at your home or place of business. As a result, it can much more easily and repeatedly be referenced.

This guidebook has been written in an alphabetical format similar to what you would find in a dictionary or an encyclopedia. As a result, the terms which are identified can very easily be looked up.

As you look through this guidebook you will see that I have divided it into ten chapters. Understanding and subsequently applying the few fairly detailed terms which are **capitalized** and appear in **bold print** in Chapter One is absolutely essential to the future success of your business. Ignore them and you may as well forget about not only staying in business for any length of time, but, ever having the opportunity to add future retail or restaurant locations. In short, they are the real "keys" to selecting what I like to call "home run" locations.

The words which are described in Chapter Two play a very strong support role in making "smart" location and "smart" site selection decisions. Understanding them will increase the probability that your business will turn out to be a success story. Collectively, these important words comprise what I like to call **primary site selection variables**.

Chapter Three contains a significant number of terms. While simply described they should not be dismissed as being unimportant. Each of these words plays a valuable support role in the site selection decision-making process. As such, I look upon them as being **secondary site selection variables**.

Chapter Four identifies the many, many **different types of locations** which exist—some of which you will end up investigating during the site selection process. While some types of locations definitely offer more advantages than others they are not listed in any hierarchy. This is because certain types of locations might be perfect for some business uses but not for others.

Chapter Five includes far and away the greatest number of terms, or, what I prefer to call **information nuggets.** There is really no way to adequately classify the significant number of terms which are described. Suffice it to say that some offer technical advice while others are approached from a common sense perspective. There is no doubt, however, that they can be influential in building retail and restaurant sales and should be regarded as important contributors to the overall profitability of your business. Accordingly, they play what I like to think of as a very significant **tangential role** in the future success of your business.

Chapters Six, Seven, Eight and Nine contain four very important **illustrative items**: How to Estimate Retail and Restaurant Sales, Creating A Site Selection Scorecard, The Importance of Demographics and Psychographics, and, Short Form and Long Form Customer Surveys.

Chapter Ten explains the most popular and arguably least understood phrase in real estate: **Location, Location, Location.** Whether you are a member of the real estate profession, a small business person, or an entrepreneur with the desire to start your own business, it is absolutely essential that you understand that while the same word is being repeated three times each word means something different. If that sounds confusing don't be alarmed. You're not alone!

Briefly, each and every business owner needs to be able to develop a system for projecting future sales. In addition, understanding anything and everything there is to know about customers as well as surrounding trade area characteristics is critical. And last, but by no means least, learning how to evaluate and subsequently rate individual sites is important. If you choose to ignore any of these items then be forewarned: you are gambling with the future success of your business.

Before proceeding further it is necessary to offer a few words of caution, especially to the many people who are use to looking for shortcuts. It would be a mistake to rely solely on the terms which are identified in Chapter One when conducting your site evaluations. Similarly, it would be a big mistake to depend primarily upon the contents of Chapter Two for direction. While these chapters collectively form a strong foundation for making informed decisions, the real value of this book lies in being able to recognize and understand the comprehensive nature of the site selection process. As such, you will find yourself much better educated and much wiser if you **read through the entirety of my book**.

There are two very important **caveats** that you need to know about prior to making a decision to open a business. The first has to do with build out and improvements. Remember that it costs the same amount of money to finish space and to purchase and install FF&E (Furniture, Fixtures and Equipment) in a good location as it does to complete your build out and install FF&E in an average or a poor location. If you plan on staying in business for a long time and you are looking forward to maximizing your return on investment then it is an absolute "no brainer" that you should focus your efforts, your energy, and your money on finding and securing only one type of location—the "home run" location!

The second **caveat** is even more important to remember. If there were one "secret" to site selection success it would be **good operations**. Indeed, nothing, I repeat nothing, not lack of visibility, inadequate parking, or poor ingress and egress, etc. is capable of making or breaking a location faster than poor operations.

Each chapter of my book can be read as a stand alone chapter. As a result, if you decide that you would like to read one or more chapters in a different order than they appear please feel free to do so. That's perfectly OK.

In conclusion, I hope that you will come to the realization that making "smart" location and "smart" site selection decisions is much more akin to running a marathon than it is to running a sprint. Unfortunately, completing the extensive preparation that goes into a marathon isn't something everyone is willing to commit to. There are lots of people who have only prepared themselves for a sprint. Consequently, many of them will see their businesses become casualties within a relatively short period of time. What an unfortunate waste of two precious resources: time and money.

I hope you enjoy reading the information which is contained in the **ABC's of Site Selection.** And, I would like to take this opportunity to wish you the best of luck in applying the information which it contains.

# CHAPTER ONE

---

# The **Six Keys** To Making "Smart" Site Selection Decisions

Throughout my real estate career I have tried to be a "quick study" as a result of continuously asking the people with whom I was working a series of questions starting with why? The answers which they provided gave me a good understanding for the processes which were used in order to make "smart" site selection decisions and reinforced what I already knew: there are no short cuts.

The six keys which follow should be committed to memory as soon as possible. If you do so, I can guarantee you that you will be saving yourself a lot of time, a lot of anguish, and, a lot of money.

**ACCESS.** Every business needs to be easily accessible to its customers. Today's consumers demand convenience. Sites which are hard to get into or out of will not only end up jeopardizing repeat business but will have a strong negative impact upon both customer counts and sales volumes. As a result, the likelihood of your business succeeding will be greatly diminished!

When you visit a prospective business site make sure that you **get out of your car and walk around**. Then, start recording your observations either with a recorder or on paper. In addition, taking a series of photographs from different vantage points is recommended. Start by counting how many curb cuts there are and exactly where they are located in relationship to the space or the property which you are interested in leasing or buying. In addition, you should note whether they accommodate full or limited turning movements.

Be careful about choosing a site which is restricted exclusively to right turns in and right turns out. Unless you are planning on opening a destination type business—one where convenience is not an important factor in generating customer traffic—such access will definitely reduce the number of people who visit your business.

The presence of a median—a barrier which can severely restrict turning movements into and out of a site—is a potential danger signal. As such, a location which has thirty thousand vehicles a day driving by may realistically find itself directly accessible to only fifty percent of that number. This means that potential customer counts are likely to be diminished by a similar amount. Remember that **reduced traffic** results in **reduced sales**. And, reduced sales typically means reduced profits.

Many busy streets and roads incorporate exclusive middle turn lanes. These are customer friendly and are an attractive, safe, and effective means of prompting increased levels of customer visits.

Another important observation you need to make is whether traffic stacks (meaning it backs up) in front of one or more of the curb cuts which serve the site you are evaluating. If a traffic stack does exist—especially during non rush hour periods—then you should either cut your site visit short or proceed with extreme caution.

**ACTIVITY.** Land uses such as shopping centers, office buildings, post offices, hotels/motels, schools, libraries, churches, grocery stores, drugstores, bookstores, cinemas, hospitals, amusement parks, banks, convenience stores, gas stations, and restaurants all have something in common—they create activity. And, activity is what generates potential customer traffic.

Determining whether or not activity exists in the immediate as well as the nearby business area you are considering appears, on the surface, to be a fairly simple exercise. However, depending upon when—meaning what the time of day or evening you visit—you will experience different levels of activity. Therefore, in order to be as informed as possible, it is very important that you make a series of location and site visits rather than relying on a single visit. Furthermore, you are advised to make your location and site visits on weekdays as well as on weekends.

When conducting your visits it is important to understand that you aren't looking exclusively for motor vehicle activity. Rather, you are trying to determine whether a high, medium, or low level of customer activity is also present. Are businesses like retail stores, restaurants, lending institutions, convenience stores, bookstores, grocery stores, and drugstores busy? Are their parking lots full or half full or not very full?

Making your observations and impressions either in writing or via voice recording is highly recommended. Please do not try to remember everything that you see—especially if you are trying to record your thoughts a few days after you make one or more field visits. Remember there is no time like the present. Otherwise remind yourself that the human mind tends to fairly quickly forget a lot of detail—something which you cannot afford to do when making an informed decision is your primary objective.

While two heads are sometimes better than one your initial site visit should not include any company. This is a time for you to focus your efforts on making and recording observations rather than on talking with a family member, another businessperson, a friend, or a trusted advisor. Each of them can become a distraction—something you cannot afford to have happen. Instead, it is recommended that you invite people whose advice you respect to accompany you once you have substantially completed your homework and have narrowed your choices to one or two potential sites.

**PARKING.** A lack of parking or inconveniently situated parking can turn out to be the "kiss of death" for most businesses, especially in suburban settings where people are extremely dependent upon the automobile in order to get around. Here, off-street surface parking is king—something which has become not only ubiquitous but has increasingly become a dominant element in the suburban landscape.

Customers typically like to find off-street and on-street parking spaces which are located either close to or reasonably close to the front door of a retail store or restaurant. In many instances this means providing as many parking spaces as possible within one hundred feet of the front door of a particular business. Parking which is located more than three hundred feet away from a business is typically taboo unless such a business is located either in a pedestrian friendly destination environment such as a lifestyle center or in a popular mixed use neighborhood.

Businesses which are freestanding can, in most instances, accommodate not only the greatest number of parking spaces but the most convenient parking for customers. Here, customer parking can be situated in front, in back, and potentially on both sides of a building. Maximizing customer parking opportunities out front or on the side of the building which is located closest to the front door is advisable rather than locating any significant amount of parking in the back.

End cap shopping center locations are also prized by businesses because customer parking can typically be accommodated not only in the front but on one side of a building. On the other hand, in line shopping center locations are pretty much restricted to providing required parking in a single area—out front.

In urban areas where neighborhood business districts tend to predominate, the fact that limited on-site parking exists means that conveniently situated on street parallel or angled parking is absolutely essential. In order to encourage use by prospective customers these parking spaces should either be free or cost relatively little. Unfortunately, metered parking can sometimes result in the issuance of a traffic ticket—a scenario which does not bode well for building either repeat customer trips or customer loyalty.

Garage and deck parking is not only very expensive to build, but isn't always customer or employee friendly. Cost is certainly the most prohibitive factor. However, concern for safety can also raise some eyebrows. Yet, garage and deck parking is vital to many businesses that are located in suburban lifestyle centers, upscale malls, neighborhood business districts which are surrounded by high density populations, and downtown areas. Without a garage or a parking deck the ability of businesses to attract a steady flow of customers would not only be limited but would result in irreparable harm.

Generally speaking, all retail and restaurant businesses need to locate as much customer parking as possible, whether it is located on or off the street, within one hundred feet of their front doors. Unless a street scene looks to be interesting, inviting, and safe, or, people are spending time going from one business to another, only a limited number of people will choose to walk very far from where they have parked. In commercial real estate, the rule of thumb is no more than three hundred feet—the length of a football field.

Different parking requirements exist for different types of businesses. Restaurants and sports bars require a ton of parking in order to adequately accommodate both customer and employee parking. Sometimes they can require as much as 15-20 parking spaces per 1,000 square feet of floor area.

Beauty salons are another example of parking intensive uses. For the most part, 5 parking spaces per 1,000 square feet of floor area is adequate for retail and service retail businesses.

In all instances, employee parking should be separated from customer parking. In particular, employee parking should be restricted to only those locations which have the least convenience appeal to customers. Generally this means that employee parking needs to be located either in back of a shopping center, on the street a required distance away, in a distant part of a parking lot, or in a nearby parking garage or parking deck.

The lack of parking in urban areas can definitely have a negative impact on retail and restaurant sales. Unfortunately, too many businesspeople overlook the lack of convenient customer parking because the property they are interested in renting or purchasing is cheap or has some other attribute such as architectural character, attractive colors, lots of windows, significant signing, etc. that they find appealing. Don't make this mistake! If a reasonable amount of parking isn't nearby then you should definitely proceed with caution.

To really comprehend the importance of conveniently situated parking you need to think about how much each parking space represents in sales. For example, does each parking space generate $15,000, $20,000, $25,000 or more in annual sales? Conveniently situated parking is money in the bank. Generally speaking, the more you have the greater your sales will typically be. Similarly, the more parking spaces you have the higher your return on investment is likely to be.

**SIGNING.** While almost every small businessperson I know of thinks that the number of signs and their sizes—the more-the-better philosophy—are the real secret to generating customer traffic their importance cannot be overlooked. Signs are definitely helpful. Indeed, they play an essential role in creating not only business identity but in helping build name recognition.

Every business, regardless of its location, should feature front facade signing that can be seen from at least one hundred to two hundred feet away. Zoning regulations in the community where you are opening your business will regulate the size, total sign area, and placement of your sign(s). In addition, some property owners may also place restrictions on signs. Hopefully neither will tie your hands with respect to colors and materials. However, if your business is located in an older or historic business district then you may well need to comply with certain restrictions.

Facade signing, whether mounted flush to or projecting from a building and whether in an older urban area or in a newer suburban location, represents your best option for displaying identification signing. Due to space limitations a business will typically only have room for its name. In other instances a business will be able to feature a symbol. In a best case scenario a sign may also be permitted to display a brief message.

If your business is located in either a freestanding building or an end cap location, chances are pretty good that additional facade signing opportunities will be available on one or both sides of a building. Based upon local zoning codes such signing will almost always be smaller than the front facade signing which is permitted.

Oftentimes, freestanding buildings also have the advantage of being able to display freestanding or pylon signs either near or at the edge of the street right of way. The only caveats here are to make sure that such signing isn't the same height as neighboring signs and is set back a little further, perhaps five to seven to ten feet, than the other freestanding or pylon signs which line the same street. In order to maximize visibility and avoid getting lost in the crowd, such signing should be easily recognized by motorists from a minimum distance of two hundred to three hundred feet away in one or more directions.

Where multi-tenant signing opportunities exist, businesses are typically able to reserve a sign panel to advertise their presence. Because little or no variation exists in panel size your best bet is to differentiate your business by making your sign stand out. Certain colors, such as red and yellow, attract more attention throughout the day and evening than others. For proof of this look no further than McDonald's and Wendy's. Their signs are not only easily recognized, but easy to remember.

As for positioning, try reserving a sign panel which is located either at the top or the bottom of the multi-tenant sign. People driving by a site tend to look at the top or the bottom of a sign which has multiple businesses identified. As such, you should make every effort to insure that your sign won't be buried somewhere in the middle—a place where it is guaranteed to get very little notice.

Individual sign letters which are capable of being lighted, whether mounted on a raceway or on the building itself, are very effective. While neon signs are more expensive, they are also very appealing. Plus, they really stand out. This is exactly what you want! On the other hand, the least attractive, least expensive, and most unimaginative building signs available for fabrication are box signs. If you are looking to maximize your image and can spend a little more money you are advised to stay away from this type of signing.

When starting work on your sign package please don't overlook the opportunity to add one or more window signs. While such signs tend to be small, they are typically very affordable. Incorporating one or more symbols or messages in your windows is an especially effective means of building name recognition for your business as well as promoting the products you sell.

**TRAFFIC.** Every business needs traffic going by its front door. Put into perspective, more is better than some, and some is better than a little. Many city and county engineers as well as metropolitan planning organizations can provide you with current or relatively current traffic count information.

Traffic volumes will be higher on primary arteries than on either collector or local streets. Whereas ten thousand vehicles a day might be adequate to support some businesses, others might require that a minimum of twenty thousand vehicles a day drive by their front door. Typically, streets and roads with these kinds of traffic volumes are two lanes—one in either direction.

A site where thirty thousand or even forty thousand vehicles a day go by may sound like an ideal situation. However, you should remember that the key is not so much the quantity of traffic but the *quality* of traffic. You need to ask yourself if the people who are driving by the site you are looking at can get in and out easily as well as safely? Typically, four lane streets and roads featuring two lanes in either direction carry these high volumes of traffic.

Other important observations you want to make when evaluating your prospective site(s) include the posted speed limit, proximity to nearby streets, the presence of medians, and whether or not a traffic signal is located close by. All of these have the potential for either negatively or positively impacting customer counts.

**VISIBILITY. No single site selection factor is more important than visibility**. Nothing, I repeat, nothing could be more accurate than the oft stated phrase "out of sight, out of mind."

Visibility is something a site either has or doesn't have. Those with lots of direct visibility as well as visibility from two hundred to three hundred feet away have a much higher probability of succeeding than sites with some or only limited visibility. Sites with no visibility are the "kiss of death." They should be avoided at all costs.

In strip shopping center settings the most desirable and most expensive sites are building pads (out lots) and end caps. One of the reasons for their popularity is their heightened visibility. The least desired and cheapest spaces on the other hand are typically in line spaces, in part because they can be largely indistinguishable from their immediate and nearby neighbor businesses, especially when located in large, multi-tenant shopping center buildings.

While facade and sign visibility are absolutely essential, parking visibility is also important. Collectively this trio of factors represents a package of impressions which can either "make or break" a site. The ideal is for all of these factors to enjoy high marks for visibility.

Sometimes street trees can block storefront and sign visibility. In other instances, trees which are planted in landscape islands in parking lots can have the same negative impact. In such instances, businesspeople need to be vigilant if good site visibility is to be retained and potentially maximized.

In certain cases, slope can negatively affect visibility. Sites that sit a little higher than the street do not generally present a visibility problem. On the other hand, sites that sit more than a few feet lower than the street generally represent an insurmountable obstacle to visibility even if their roofs are easily seen.

Distance and timing are two other important ways of determining the amount of visibility a business enjoys. Typically, the further away from the street a business is located the less visible it will be. Similarly, the longer the period of time that a person sees a business while driving by it, the better.

Another means of evaluating visibility has to do with storefront windows, glass wrap, and walls. Both of the former are great ways to welcome customers and increase visibility. On the other hand, large expanses of walls on the side and front of a building can turn off and turn away customers—something no business can afford.

In older business districts, storefront differentiation is an important means of increasing visibility—something today's lifestyle centers have been quick to copy. Here, different building materials, recessed entryways, appealing colors, bay windows, nighttime lighting and customized awnings are great ways to not only create a unique and more memorable identity but to increase storefront visibility.

---

A fun way to remember all of the six keys which have been identified is to create a simple system. For instance, if you choose to remember them in alphabetical order you can classify them into the following pairs: AA, PS, and TV. Otherwise you might classify them into three different groups of very short words such AS, AT, and VP or AS, PA, and TV. If you prefer, you can even separate them into two groups of three letters, like PSA and TVA or ATV and SAP. Perhaps the easiest way to remember the six keys, however, is to create an acronym or a word which is followed by one or more letters. For example **PASTA V** or PAST VA.

Your immediate goal is to focus as much of your attention as possible on the combination of the six keys in order to establish a strong foundation for future business success. If the site which you are considering does not satisfy all of these criteria then you should redirect your efforts to other potential business addresses. Alternatively, if each of these important factors has been satisfied, you are ready to proceed to the next step: evaluating the influence which primary and secondary site selection variables will have on future sales.

Satisfying the six keys as well as both the primary and secondary variables will provide you with the confirmation that you are on the right path—one which will substantially improve the odds of your achieving long term business success.

# Chapter Two

## Primary Site Selection Factors

**Adjacencies.** Not enough businesspeople pay attention to who their next door neighbors are. This can be a serious oversight and can result in not only lost revenues, but business failure. If you are contemplating opening a restaurant next door to a beauty salon you could be making a terrible mistake. This is because both businesses will likely be competing for the same valuable customer parking spaces.

Other potential adjacency problems can arise if two neighboring businesses aren't compatible. For instance, someone who is contemplating opening up a restaurant should avoid a location which is next door to a pet store. Similarly, if you are thinking about opening up a children's boutique you should be careful about choosing a location next to a bar or tavern.

**Anchors.** These are the businesses which not only drive customer traffic to a particular location, but also help to attract other businesses. They can be big box stores, mall stores, grocery stores, drugstores, bookstores, toy stores, office supply stores, and even destination restaurants.

Some anchors, like grocery stores and drugstores, will generate weekly customer traffic. Others, like malls, will generate less frequent customer visits. Regardless of how often a customer is likely to visit a retail or restaurant anchor the bottom line is that their ability to increase customer traffic counts will positively impact customer counts for your business.

**Area Hours of Operation.** When conducting your fieldwork make sure that you know which area businesses are open early and which remain open late. If you are counting on evening traffic to generate customers and you are the only retailer in the area who is open during the evening then you should count on attracting fewer shoppers to your store.

Understanding when prospective customers are in the area where you are located will enable you to not only make more informed site selection decisions but allow you to get a better handle on estimating future sales.

**Barriers, Physical & Psychological.** From a physical standpoint, Interstate highways, hills, rivers, and large expanses of undeveloped land often negatively impact both the size and shape of customer trade areas. Individually or collectively they create a real divide. As a result, any businessperson or prospective businessperson should be aware of their presence and their ability to inhibit customer traffic and sales.

Many psychological barriers, such as different levels of street lighting, a change in the character and physical condition of the buildings lining a street, racial composition, income levels, lack of conveniently situated parking, the high cost of parking, crime levels, and a change in political jurisdictions, are individually and collectively potential impediments to the success of a business.

Such barriers can get lost in the statistical data which is found in a demographic report. This is where data appearing in demographic map form can create a much clearer picture of the population living in the surrounding area. However, even as informative as a demographic map is it should ideally be accompanied by psychographic data. Understanding lifestyle segmentation data is essential to making more informed and better site selection decisions.

While demographic data and maps, along with psychographic data, provides a significant amount of meaningful information, there is no substitute for not only completing one or more site visits but conducting detailed site and surrounding area evaluations. Relying on data and maps in lieu of site visits and evaluations is tantamount to "rolling the dice."

**Building Setback.** With the exception of large retail anchor stores, the closer a business is located to the street the better. This is especially true of businesses which cater to the convenience crowd. Good examples of such businesses are bakeries, dry cleaners, and sandwich shops.

Too often businesspeople fail to take into consideration the fact that prospective customers are looking at signs as their primary means of finding a particular business. If you were to put yourself in the shoes of a prospective customer which of the following building sign distances would end up being the most visible to you: those which are located one hundred, two hundred, or three hundred feet off the road?

**Compatibility.** When making a location decision please make sure that your business fits well with neighboring businesses. What you want to strive to be a part of is a good tenant mix, one where businesses can easily coexist and no business is detrimental to its neighbors or to nearby businesses.

Hours of operation, parking, and types of businesses are all important components of compatibility. In certain instances, compatibility will lead to one or more businesses sharing customers. This, in turn, will result in increased sales revenues for each business.

**Competition.** Knowing who your competition is, what their price points are, what they have to offer, how their site stacks up, and why they are successful is important information. Even more important, however, is knowing who their customers are and what their sales volumes are.

Remember that while it is easy to identify who your competition is it is much more difficult to understand what impact they will have on your sales. Since the opportunity exists to share some of the same customers make sure that you periodically monitor your competition.

**Connectivity.** The more ways there are for customers to reach your retail store or restaurant the easier and more convenient it will be for you to capture their business. While locating your business on a busy commercial corridor is desirable, the ideal is to find a site on a busy street which is served by two or more nearby intersecting streets. This is what will potentially provide you with a competitive advantage.

If your business is located too far off the street, typically more than approximately one hundred and fifty feet, or, is located in either a large multi-tenant shopping center or a long row of businesses where little or no storefront differentiation occurs, being either close to or near a street intersection will not be of any real benefit. Indeed, excessive setbacks and getting lost in a crowd are two factors which can lead to an increased risk of business failure.

**Critical Mass.** The overall size and extent of the business district which surrounds your site is important. Typically, you want to locate your business in an area where there are two or more reasons for people to be out and around. Being able to go to the drugstore and the dry cleaner, or perhaps the video store, the gas station, the bank, or your favorite pizza carry out in one trip represents a huge savings of time.

In order to increase your chances for business success look for locations in areas which are surrounded by not only a mix of businesses and land uses, but which include one or more retail or restaurant anchors. The benefits which are attributable to such locations include increased name recognition as well as increased customer traffic. Unless you are contemplating opening either a convenience store or a gasoline business you should definitely avoid being a pioneer—the first business to open in an area.

**Curb Appeal.** Simply stated, most people will recognize it when they see it. If curb appeal exists count yourself fortunate. If it doesn't you are automatically positioning yourself behind "the eight ball." From attractive entryways to appealing landscaping to easy to read signing to functional windows to colorful awnings, curb appeal is one of the most overlooked and least understood criteria in the site selection decision making process.

Business owners spend the great majority of their time inside their stores and restaurants. As a result, making outdoor-related observations can be challenging. However, the opposite is true of prospective customers. They are more than willing to judge a book by its cover. If your business has some, little, or no curb appeal you are restricting opportunities for building customer traffic. Consequently, you need to spend more time thinking about ways to enhance your curb appeal in order to do the most fundamental thing of all—attracting both first time and repeat customers.

**Customer Profile Information.** When you are searching for a location you should have a thorough understanding of who your customers are and where they will be coming from. If you are the operator of an existing business you should already possess this important information. In instances where you are contemplating buying a franchise make sure that the prospective franchisor provides you with such information. If the franchisor can't, then you are advised to find out why not?

If you are opening a start-up business as opposed to taking over an existing business you have the disadvantage of not having any customer profile information. In such instances the best information regarding potential customers will come from knowing who is buying from your primary competitor(s).

Without having some knowledge of existing or future customers you need to understand that you will be assuming a greater degree of risk with respect to the future success of your business location.

**Data Collection.** Anybody who is contemplating opening a new business needs to not only obtain site specific demographic information, but learn about such other factors as a location's rental and common area costs, occupancy and vacancy levels, and traffic counts. Where a business already has a customer profile, obtaining psychographic data (lifestyle information) is also recommended.

**Daytime Population.** The focus here is on understanding as much as possible about the population which works within the trade area serving your business as opposed to the population which lives in the surrounding trade area. Daytime demographics play a very important role in supporting certain types of businesses. For example, convenience oriented businesses such as quick service (fast food) restaurants, gas stations, and banks are good candidates to attract steady business from daytime workers in the nearby area.

Keep in mind that different types of employers will have different hours of operation. For example, some businesses might restrict the amount of time which is available for employee lunches to thirty minutes while others may allow an hour.

While some employers will have low pay levels others may provide higher paying jobs. Some businesses may employ more women than men. The point is, don't assume that every nearby daytime worker is alike and represents the same "capture" opportunity for your business.

Obtaining current as well as reliable daytime information can prove to be challenging. This is why talking to commercial realtors, landlords, and commercial developers is very important. Similarly, you should count on making visits to individual businesses, to City Hall, and to the local Chamber of Commerce. And, don't overlook the need to conduct fieldwork. It is absolutely vital.

**Demographics.** It is important to be able to collect and evaluate a variety of current or relatively recent statistical information. Examples include total population, income levels, education levels, job types, daytime population, and home values. One critical recommendation is to **always concentrate on numbers as opposed to percentages.**

While ring demographics (for instance one-three-five miles) are most frequently used because they make an easy "apples to apples" comparison, my preference is to order drive time demographics. My experience is that very few people will be able to tell you how far they drove or walked to your business. However, most of them will quickly be able to inform you that their drive or walk took them three, five, or ten minutes.

While obtaining this type of data is essential, it is important to understand that demographics are nothing more than a starting point. In other words, don't let demographics be the dominant influence in where you decide to locate your business. A location with outstanding demographics is only as good as its operator and the combination of the site related factors which are identified in chapter one.

**Density.** The more people who live and work in a particular area the greater the likelihood is that your business will be able to capture increased customer traffic. Higher density areas—whether they are comprised of residential, retail, restaurant, and/or office—can definitely be a boost to customer sales. Consequently, density should be taken into consideration during the early stages as opposed to the later stages of the site selection process.

Differences in density are most apparent as you transition from urban to suburban to rural areas. In urban environments people may have many, many choices within a five minute walk or drive time. In suburban areas they may have lots of choices within a ten minute drive time. In rural areas they may have only a few choices and may need to drive fifteen or more minutes in order to visit stores, restaurants, banks, etc. As such it is important to remember that as density increases the size of individual trade areas typically shrink.

**Depth of Space.** Ideally, for every three feet of depth, a store or a restaurant should have one foot of frontage. Thus, a twenty foot wide storefront should have a maximum depth of sixty feet. This ratio is important because narrow, deep space is not only less functional for most businesses, but is much less desirable from a customer perspective.

By all means, you should avoid the bowling alley look when you are out shopping for retail or restaurant space. Such a look starts at and oftentimes exceeds a ratio of four feet of depth for every one foot of frontage. While the rent for such elongated space will definitely be less than the rent for conventionally shaped space, the bottom line is that it is by far the least desirable space available.

**Drive Thru Window.** Having a drive thru window at many restaurants is an important customer convenience—especially in suburban settings. Indeed, in order to remain competitive, quick service (fast food) restaurants need to feature this important amenity—especially since they can routinely account for sixty percent or more of overall sales.

Drive thru windows are different from pick up windows because they require customers to select food and beverage items from a menu board prior to the receipt of their orders. Thus, customers typically need to wait in line, both before and after placing their orders.

One word of caution: make sure that a bypass traffic lane exists so that customers who decide they want to leave a long line of slow moving vehicles can do just that as opposed to finding themselves stuck in line.

**Drive Times.** It is very important that you know about and understand the extent of both your primary and secondary customer trade areas. Driving times rather than driving distances (for example, one, two, or three miles) provide a very important insight into how far your customers are willing to travel in order to patronize you.

For most suburban businesses, the critical drive times are typically five to seven to ten minutes. In urban areas your drive times are likely to shrink a little while in rural areas they are likely to increase. As for walking, most people will only walk about three to five minutes in order to get to their destination. If they happen to go bar hopping or decide to visit a pedestrian friendly shopping area the time they spend walking will increase but not significantly.

Unlike ring demographics, drive time demographics tell us a lot about a very important factor—convenience. The importance of this element should not be lost on business owners unless they operate what can unequivocally be classified as a destination type business. Businesses such as cinemas, jewelry stores, pubs, bookstores, and specialty and/or higher end restaurants qualify to wear such a mantle. However, they represent a significant minority of the businesses which populate our cities, towns, villages, and unincorporated areas.

**Fieldwork.** This is an activity where many businesspeople as well as most prospective businesspeople earn a failing grade. Simply stated, devoting hours and hours to not only making site and trade area visits but recording your observations is critical to understanding the pros and cons of a particular site and location. As the late, great Hall of Fame and former UCLA basketball coach John Wooden was fond of saying: "failure to prepare is preparing to fail."

Visits and observations should be made during morning, noon, and nighttime hours not only during weekdays but on weekends. During these site visits try talking with as many tenants and business owners as possible. In addition, don't be shy about calling such resource parties as the leasing or sales agent for the property, local governmental authorities, transportation officials, etc. Field trips represent a great opportunity to not only gather information, but to "leave no stone unturned."

**Frontage.** Whether you are looking at street frontage, building frontage, or window frontage, make sure you memorize these four words: "the more the better." Retail and restaurant space which contains minimum amounts of frontage, especially those with excessive depth, should be avoided at all costs! A good standard to keep in mind is three to one—a maximum of three feet of building depth for every one foot of frontage.

**Going Home Side of the Street.** For many businesses this is the preferred side of the street to be located on. Grocery stores, workout facilities, gas stations, liquor stores, and carryout pizza restaurants are some of the many businesses which benefit from "intercepting" customers on their way home.

**Going to Work Side of the Street.** If you are in the coffee, doughnut, or breakfast sandwich business, it is imperative that you pick a location on the going to work side of the street. Being able to offer customers the opportunity to make a quick right turn into and out of your business is a convenience factor which will end up enhancing sales.

**Ingress and Egress.** In Chapter One access is discussed. Access is all about being able to get into and out of a site both conveniently and safely. Typically, convenience and safety are influenced by the number and placement of curb cuts. If "easy in, easy out" isn't characteristic of the location you are considering then you are advised not to waste any more of your valuable time.

**Location Location Location.** These are three of the most complex, widely used, and misunderstood words in the site selection business. Ignore them and you assume an increased risk of failure. Master them and success is much more likely.

The key here is to think of location as a bundle of many different factors as opposed to a single factor. Approached in this manner, you will devote a significant amount of time and energy to data collection and fieldwork—something which will enable you to make more informed location decisions. As a result of doing an extensive amount of homework, you can be confident that you are on the road to making "smart" location decisions.

In my mind Location Location Location stands for three types of locations: "Grand Slam" locations, "Home Run" locations, and "Triple" locations. Think of them as being A+, A, and B+ locations. The first two types are the hardest locations to come by. Yet, they are exactly the types of locations which consistently help define McDonald's and Walgreen's and other highly successful companies. Another way to describe them is "100% locations"—the bluest of the blue. Few and far between they are, quite simply, the best of the best, the cream of the crop!

**Market Research.** Please reference Data Collection, Demographics, Fieldwork, and Psychographics.

**Median Strips.** Avoid not only evaluating, but selecting sites where these types of physical barriers exist. They are literally "the kiss of death" when it comes to attracting customer traffic. Remember, one mistake in site selection can realistically make the difference between success and failure.

**Nighttime Population.** This important term refers to the resident population which lives in a particular area. It is one of the first and one of the most important factors which needs to be evaluated in the site selection process.

Typically, the more rooftops which surround a potential business site the better. Rooftops are especially important to restaurants which attract a significant amount of dinner business. A pizza restaurant is a prime example. Whether it offers customers dine in service or focuses on pick up and delivery, rooftops are essential to generating high levels of customer traffic as well as repeat business.

The nighttime population is the focus of most demographic reports. These reports provide existing as well as prospective businesspeople, consultants, and commercial realtors with detailed information and projections which are based upon the most recent Census of Population. Whether reported by political jurisdiction, drive times, radii, or zip code, such data is essential to understanding the characteristics of the people who live in the surrounding trade area.

**Parallel vs. Perpendicular Building Space**. Always look for a location which sits parallel to the street. Parallel buildings are not only more visible to motorists and pedestrians than buildings which sit perpendicular to the street, but are also more inviting to them. While every tenant in a parallel building will face the street, with the exception of end cap or corner locations, buildings which sit perpendicular to the street will provide substantially less visibility.

Never, ever let cheap rent for a space in a building which sits perpendicular to the street become a factor in making your location decision. While space in a building which sits parallel to the street will almost always cost you more, the bottom line is that it will end up generating higher sales levels—something which could end up making the difference between your staying in business or going out of business.

When you think about these two types of buildings make a simple apples and oranges comparison. In this case the apples are parallel sitting buildings and the oranges are perpendicular sitting buildings. Don't forget this comparison—that's how different they are from one another!

Some shopping center developments with one or more large anchor tenants will periodically violate **the parallel is preferred rule** and build "B" shop space which sits perpendicular to the street in order to accommodate a cluster of small to mid size tenants. While these types of shopping centers are frequently able to attract and keep a stable mix of tenants, their success is largely attributable to being located in close proximity to one or more anchors. Therefore, they represent the exception rather the rule.

When you think about it, when is the last time you remember seeing an anchor store which sits perpendicular as opposed to parallel to the street? The answer is very, very seldom. As such, why wouldn't you want to make the same type of site selection decision?

**Pickup Window.** An increasing number of businesses are incorporating pickup windows in the end caps of their buildings and space in order to provide additional convenience for their customers—the great majority of whom call ahead and place their orders.

Unlike drive thru windows, pick up windows do not require either a menu board or a speaker system. Consequently, they are much less likely to have a line of cars, trucks, SUVs and mini vans waiting to get their food and/or drinks.

**Psychographics.** This is a word which is unfamiliar to a lot of people but should not remain a mystery for any length of time. Psychographics look at consumers from a lifestyle perspective. They provide businesses with an opportunity to gain a deep understanding about the people who live in a trade area.

Psychographics segment households into different lifestyle groups. PRIZM, which is published by Claritas, describes a total of sixty-six different lifestyle groups. As such, it is an extremely powerful tool for understanding a great deal about consumer behavior on a microscale as opposed to the macroscale which characterizes demographic reports.

Psychographics provide business owners and prospective businesspeople with an unparalleled opportunity to understand who their customers are, where they live, where they shop, where they eat, what their ages and education levels are, what they read, what types of housing they live in, what types of jobs they have, what their income levels are, etc., etc.

PRIZM ranks its lifestyle groups and assigns each of them an interesting name. For instance, the most prestigious consumer group, ranked number one, is known as Upper Crust. Movers and Shakers and Country Squires round out the Top Three. Some other interesting lifestyle groups include Pools & Patios, Gray Power, Urban Achievers, and Young Digerati.

**Safety.** If the neighborhood you're looking at isn't safe, then don't waste your time looking for retail or restaurant space, even if the asking price is right. Safety can be a tremendous influence on sales, especially whenever women constitute a large percentage of your customers.

One of the best crime deterrents is lighting—whether it is located on a building or in a parking lot. Another important deterrent is the amount of nighttime activity in both the immediate and surrounding areas, whether pedestrian or vehicular.

**Sales Estimates/Forecasts.** Sales estimates need to be done well in advance of either signing a lease agreement or purchasing property. Developing a reliable system for estimating future store or restaurant sales is not an easy task. Like site selection, **sales forecasting is part art and part science**. Think of sales forecasts as the "icing on a cake." If you don't include them in your site evaluation something very important will be missing.

If you are fortunate enough to operate one or more existing businesses, you have a good platform for projecting future sales. However, this important task becomes much more complicated for the first time business person. Even though you would assume otherwise, estimating sales can be a difficult and time consuming task even for people who have purchased a franchise. This is because federal law prohibits franchisors from providing store sales advice to franchisees due to the fact that they risk misrepresenting the amount of future sales a business can do.

Knowing about or developing a customer profile can make sales forecasting not only less intimidating, but a lot less time consuming. Where such information is unavailable, you will need to do some homework starting with a determination of which variables or factors should be included in the sales forecasting methodology which will be used. For the faint of heart, turning to an experienced site selection consultant is one possible solution. Other options include speaking with an experienced business person or talking with one or more fellow franchisees.

**Site Analysis/Evaluation.** This is what separates the men from the boys. If you invest the time to do a thorough site analysis which is based upon multiple site visits, the likelihood that you will be making a much more informed location decision increases significantly.

Don't fall in love with a location based upon a first-time site visit. While first impressions are important they aren't enough to justify making a decision that represents a significant monetary investment—one which could include not only a rent or mortgage obligation but a construction loan as well as the purchase of furniture, fixtures, and equipment (FF&E).

Also, **under no circumstances should you let emotion influence your thinking**. Sadly, too many people make this mistake. Making a business location decision is much different and much more complex than buying a house. It is much more about having a system in place. For a good insight into such a system please review the Site Selection Scorecard which appears in Chapter Seven.

**Site Distance.** Too many people look at visibility from a head on perspective. In other words, they evaluate site visibility from directly in front of a particular property. Doing so should only be a starting point. What you also need to observe is visibility from approximately two and three hundred feet away. Your objective is to determine how many seconds the site you are considering is clearly visible to someone who is either stopped at a traffic signal or who is driving the speed limit. **The longer your site is visible the better.**

Too often what impairs clear and sustained visibility is slope, other buildings, and trees and shrubs. At a minimum you want the sites which you are considering to be clearly visible to the driving public for a minimum of four to five seconds. This is usually a long enough time frame for someone to not only read your sign but to deposit your business name in their memory bank.

**Site Grade.** Flat or relatively flat sites are the only types of sites that you want to spend time evaluating. Be especially cautious when looking at sites which sit more than a few feet below street level. Otherwise, you will sacrifice visibility, especially signing visibility—something which you cannot afford to do!

Slightly elevated sites—those which sit no more than a few feet above street level—are also worthy of your consideration.

In the long run you want to secure sites whose grades do *not* exceed six or seven percent of slope (as measured over a distance of one hundred feet). Sites which exceed this time honored standard risk creating not only unpleasant uphill and downhill walks for their customers but the prospect of having to deal with potential drainage problems.

**Site Selection Guidelines and Standards.** Either you have **a system for success** or you don't. Every national and the great majority of regional retail and restaurant companies rely on site selection guidelines and standards. Furthermore, they are almost always administered by an in-house real estate department. Sadly, for one reason or another, most local businesses overlook the need for these very important elements.

Site selection guidelines and standards help retail and restaurant businesses avoid mistakes. They help to explain what separates successful businesses from the not so successful and/or failed businesses. Indeed, the presence of site selection guidelines and standards is what helps to differentiate the "big boys" from the "little guys."

**Speed Limit.** The higher the speed limit on the street where you are considering opening your business the faster vehicles will drive by. The faster they drive by the less time they will have to see and remember both your storefront and your signing.

Generally speaking, streets with posted speed limits of twenty five, thirty, and thirty five miles per hour are more attractive and more viable locations than streets where the posted speed limit is higher. Ultimately, the rate of speed affects visibility. The more likely your business can be seen the more you are ahead of the curve. However, if you decide to sacrifice visibility you could find yourself behind "the eight ball" right off the bat.

**Synergy.** Finding a location where businesses compliment one another and have the potential for increasing one another's customer base and sales can be "money in the bank." Locations where two or more synergistic opportunities exist is the ideal. Nonetheless, locations with only one such opportunity are better than locations with no synergy.

The best examples of synergy at work can be found at the many regional malls which are located across the United States. Observe how women's jewelry, clothing, and shoe stores like to be next to or near one another. Why is this? The answer is because they help generate customer traffic and sales for one another.

If you are in the ice cream business, selecting a location which is near one or more restaurants—especially family-friendly pizza restaurants, a bookstore, and/or a cinema complex—can be a big boost to sales. If you are in the sandwich business, the best neighbors you can have are the other restaurants in the area and nearby places of employment. While not every employee will eat out on a regular basis, chances are they will go out to lunch at least once a week. Hopefully you can capture some of the traffic they represent.

An often overlooked but outstanding example of synergy is food and gas. The two go together hand in glove. Similarly, jewelry stores, shoe stores, clothing stores, cosmetics stores, and beauty salons can boost sales for one another.

**Trade Area.** This is the area from which a business generates the great majority of its customer traffic. It is important to point out that repeat or frequent customer visits are much more important to business success than occasional or infrequent customer visits. Also, it is necessary to differentiate between primary and secondary trade areas. The former typically comprises anywhere from sixty to seventy percent of customer traffic whereas the latter typically accounts for most, but not all, of the balance of customer traffic.

The best way to learn about the extent of an existing trade area is to invest in doing customer surveys and then mapping individual customer points of origination. In most cases people will be coming to your business from their homes. In other cases they will originate their trips from their places of employment. Other points of origin could include shopping centers, restaurants, or perhaps sports, cultural, and entertainment functions.

Most businesspeople exaggerate the extent of their customer trade areas. The simplest explanation for this is that they don't really know much about their customers. Most have never taken the time or spent the money necessary to document where, in fact, their customers are coming from or the frequency of their visits. As a result, when these businesspeople get ready to look for other locations they are unable to utilize factual site selection criteria to make important decisions.

**All successful chain retail and restaurant companies understand not only the extent of their trade areas but everything there is to know about the customers who originate from such trade areas.** Indeed, this is one of the reasons why they have been able to open either hundreds or even thousand of locations!

**Traffic Quality.** Factors such as traffic congestion, restricted turning movements, streets with a significant number of traffic lanes, frequent traffic stops, the lack of turning lanes, the opportunity to travel at high speeds, and limited or poor site access can singularly or collectively discourage or harm customer patronage.

**Traffic Signalization.** Being at or near a traffic signal is usually, but not always, a potential advantage for your business. Traffic signals typically mean that lots of traffic will be driving by your front door as a result of the critical mass (for example, large numbers of offices, retail, and restaurant businesses) which is located in the immediate area. It also means that vehicles will typically be slowing down or be stopping—something which should result not only in increased visibility but increased customer traffic.

The one caution about locating your business at or near a traffic signal is the amount of vehicle stacking which can occur. Being too close to a traffic signal may result in long lines of backed-up cars, SUV's, mini vans, and trucks—all of which can combine to prevent easy turning movements into or out of your site.

When looking at "near" corner locations (as opposed to "far" corner locations) always count the number of vehicles which are stacking during the hours when your business will be the busiest. If stacking appears to be a problem then you are advised to start looking for another location—even if everything else appears to be fine. **There is no room for gambling when it comes to site selection.** It is far better to be safe than sorry.

**Walk and Talk.** While you are making your site specific visits don't overlook the opportunity to talk with other shopping center tenants and nearby businesspeople—they can provide you with lots of good insights. One of the most important of these is how well the property you are looking at is maintained. Ask about snow removal, landscaping, and trash pick up. Also, inquire about any roof, parking lot, and/or common signing problems.

A word of caution: please do not limit yourself to making only a site specific visit. While you are in the area you should check out nearby anchors, traffic, your competition, and other potential locations for your retail and/or restaurant business. In addition, observe who is busy and who is not. And, don't forget to take lots of pictures.

**Windows.** Typically, the more windows your business has the better. If you are in the retail business you need windows for display purposes. If you are in the restaurant business you already understand that people tend to gravitate to window seats. At a minimum, eighty percent or more of your building frontage should feature glass.

Some locations feature floor to ceiling windows, others feature windows above a low wall—typically what is referred to as a knee wall. Does one type of window have an advantage over the other? The answer is probably not. However, given a choice, windows which are located above a knee wall are preferable, especially in the case of restaurants.

While front windows are absolutely essential, windows which extend along a portion of the side of an end cap space or a freestanding building will benefit some businesses, especially restaurants. Glass wrap helps to bring in more natural light and can make your business more appealing, more inviting to customers. Also, the amount of windows you have can help to differentiate your business from other businesses.

In certain instances, having a section of high glass located along the back wall of your space is recommended—especially if you are in the retail service business and are in need of some small office space, or, need more inviting customer space. For safety and privacy purposes, high glass should never be installed lower than seven feet off the ground.

Older business districts often feature recessed storefronts which are flanked on either side by display windows. They provide retail and restaurant owners with something which is critically important—additional display space. While newer strip centers almost always overlook such an important amenity, many mall stores as well as many lifestyle centers routinely incorporate these types of storefront windows into their building designs.

One word of caution: be careful to provide either an overhang or awnings for windows which face south or west. Otherwise, you will experience not only the potential for items to fade, but customers who may become uncomfortable due to heat build up. In the restaurant business this is especially critical because every seat needs to be occupied as often as possible. If the noontime, afternoon, or early evening sun is real bright, chances are good that your window seats will not be used.

Any architect, developer, or businessperson who is involved in new development needs to take the location of the sun into consideration when contemplating the design and construction of a new building. If this isn't done then what will be created will likely have a sun problem—something which could end up negatively impacting sales.

# CHAPTER THREE

## Secondary Site Selection Factors

**Amenities.** These are the "extras" that help to differentiate your location from your competitor's place of business. Examples include outdoor seating, fountains and water features, upgraded landscaping, pedestrian friendly shopping center design, and shopping center entryways which make a great first impression.

**Area Charm & Character.** Many start-up businesses place a major emphasis on an item which is absent from most shopping centers: unique, one-of-a kind storefronts. While creating something special can be challenging, it can also turn out to be very rewarding.

**Arterial Streets.** See Primary Streets.

**Basement Locations.** Unless you locate your business in an area where other retail and restaurants are consistently found below street level, you should avoid basement locations. These are highly suspect locations, primarily because of limitations on signing, windows, natural light, and an overall lack of visibility. In addition, most shoppers don't like going up and down stairs or riding elevators, especially if they are carrying one or more shopping bags or are toting one or more small children.

**Cannibalization.** This term refers to the sales transfer impact one location has on another. Whether you operate a mom-and-pop retail store or restaurant, a small chain, or, are a franchisee owned business, you should be concerned about the potential for cannibalization. Because there is no room for guessing, the best way to prevent the unwanted transfer of sales from one location to another, say no more than ten to twelve to fifteen percent, is to have a very good understanding of the extent of your existing customer trade area and who your primary customers are.

**Captive Customers.** Airports, universities, and malls are good examples of places where captive audiences exist. Here, customers are likely to find only a limited number of retail stores and restaurants. In these types of locations convenience is king and helps to explain most trip generation.

**Cheap Rent.** How many "home run" locations do you know of which are characterized by cheap rent? The answer should be very few if any! Yet, cheap rent is frequently the reason why many business locations are selected.

Rental space is typically cheap for reasons such as deferred property maintenance, lack of an anchor tenant, the need for a new HVAC system, the need to make roof repairs, little or no landlord build out contribution, excessive depth, high vacancy rates, limited signing opportunities, minimal visibility, limited or inconveniently situated parking, impaired ingress and egress, poor tenant mix, functional obsolescence, etc.

One or a combination of these drawbacks can end up costing a retail or restaurant owner something very important: customer sales. Yet, such drawbacks can be overlooked by people who have not done their homework, are overly anxious to open a new business, or, don't grasp the fact that one or more of their competitors have superior locations.

Unless you have a unique or destination business, it is important to remember that cheap rent retail and restaurant locations usually are guaranteed to produce only marginal sales. In the long run there is no getting around the fact that you get what you pay for.

**Collector Streets.** These are the types of streets which feed large amounts of traffic onto major roads, streets, and highways. While they carry a lesser amount of traffic than arterial streets, they typically generate many more cars, trucks, and SUVs than do local streets. In comparison with local streets, collector streets typically permit not only higher speed limits, but feature more moving lanes of traffic.

**Color.** Both your business and the property where you are or will be located need to stand out. Typically this can best be accomplished as a result of attractive building design, attractive and/or unique signing, attractive landscaping, the use of awnings, and, color schemes which attract lots of attention.

Two colors always command attention: red and yellow. Perhaps this explains why businesses with a worldwide presence such as McDonald's, Wendy's, and Shell feature red and yellow in all of their signs. Color, especially with respect to signs and awnings, oftentimes is responsible for creating a customer's first impression. As such, don't be shy about incorporating one or more bold colors into your storefront design as well as into the image that you want to project.

**Commercial Realtors.** One of the first resource groups whom you should contact are commercial realtors. They are typically knowledgeable about not only the availability of retail and/or restaurant space, but leasing and purchase costs, comparable real estate values, occupancy levels, demographics, traffic counts, rental and purchase costs, rent concessions, etc.

Besides having relationships with landlords, property owners, and developers, commercial realtors are typically paid commissions by these groups whenever a property is sold or leased. Thus, their services cost you nothing—they are free!

**Common Area.** This is the portion of a shopping center which is located immediately outside both the front and back doors of space which is occupied by individual tenants. It is the area which includes entryways, driveways, parking lots, sidewalks, storefront and parking lot lighting, common seating, the dumpster pad, common signing, landscaping, and water features.

**Common Area Charges.** In addition to paying your pro rata share of common area maintenance costs, pass through expenses typically include your pro rata share of real estate taxes and insurance. Collectively, these costs are oftentimes referred to as CAM charges. These costs are above and beyond the cost of your monthly rent and typically should only increase a little every year.

**Congestion.** Traffic which is regularly backed up can have a negative impact on store and/or restaurant sales. People tend to avoid locations where gridlock is a common occurrence, especially if turning movements can result in periodic accidents.

**Consultants.** Companies such as *Location Decision Advisors,* the author's site selection company, can be an invaluable resource when it comes to making "smart" location and "smart" site selection decisions. Consultants typically have years of experience assisting businesses in not just locating potential locations, but in analyzing whether or not they are what I like to call A, B, or C locations.

**Costs.** What a business can afford to pay for rent and common area charges is a direct function of sales—something which is lost on many prospective and first time businesspeople. For most businesses the combination of these two factors should represent approximately ten percent of total sales.

**Curb Cuts.** See Ingress and Egress in chapter two.

**Decay Curve.** This little-known phrase refers to the fact that as driving or walking distance from a business increases customer traffic ends up diminishing. In this case, reference is made to miles as well as minutes. You need to take this important factor into consideration when conducting your site search.

**Developers.** Many times the best way to secure a "home run" location is to work with developers. The absolute best time to meet with them is before any ground is broken for a commercial and/or mixed use development. This way you can get a better understanding of not only their concept plans but one or more location options. If you start early enough you may even be able to influence how certain amenities such as outdoor seating can be incorporated into the project in order to better serve your specific needs and requirements.

The best link to the development community is commercial realtors. For many of them new development, as opposed to existing commercial space, is a critical focus area. In many instances, they will have preestablished relationships with developers—something many small businesspeople don't. This important resource group also understands the commercial marketplace and is well positioned to provide you with the kind of negotiating tools and assistance which can lead to the creation of a win-win opportunity for both you and the developer.

**Drop Lane.** Having the opportunity to make a right hand turn into a site from a separately dedicated traffic lane extending for one hundred or more feet is not only driver friendly but a welcome safety feature.

**Education Levels.** This is both a demographic and psychographic variable which can be a very important influence in the site selection process. For upscale retail shops and restaurants the higher the education levels within a trade area the better. Conversely, the customer base for some businesses will consist primarily of customers with lower education levels.

**Egress.** Locations where it is difficult to exit, whether turning left or waiting behind a stack of cars, mini vans, SUV's, and trucks, present a potential problem. This is because if it is difficult to turn left personal safety becomes much more of a concern. In cases where traffic ends up stacking, a person's patience will be tested and, if bad enough, could result in business avoidance. The best way to mitigate these concerns is to have your site served by a traffic signal. Remember that convenience is not only the name of the game, but something which can have a profound influence on both customer traffic and customer sales.

**Entryways.** These are the "gateways" into your location. As a result, they need to stand out. Attractive, well maintained entryways heighten anticipation and create the impression that something worthwhile awaits a retail or restaurant visitor. Yet, appealing entryways are not only often overlooked, but are simply forgotten about. The ultimate loser, of course, is your small business.

**Façade Enhancements.** Making your storefront standout is an important means of not only increasing your visibility, but attracting customers. This can be accomplished in a variety of ways. Some of the most common are painting, lighting, and awnings.

**Free Rent.** This is a great way for landlords to maintain desired property valuations while providing a strong incentive for tenants to lease space. Oftentimes tenants are given free rent as a means of reducing their initial financial obligation. In other instances, landlords can provide free rent in exchange for a tenants' making a series of interior improvements ranging from upgraded HVAC and electric to extra plumbing and additional walls. In certain instances, free rent can extend to having tenants make one or more exterior improvements such as the provision of patio seating, awnings, building lighting, and facade enhancements.

The provision of free rent is an especially effective tool when a tenant's financial statement and/or credit is sub par and results in a landlord's unwillingness to invest some or any money in making one or more interior and/or exterior improvements. It is also an important incentive when a landlord is unwilling to drop his or her initial rents below a certain level but realizes that being able to lease space can't be achieved without some provision for free rent—perhaps two or three or four months of free rent.

**Front Door Parking.** If you are in the convenience business, front door customer parking is absolutely essential to attracting customers and propelling sales. How much parking is required depends upon the nature of your business and its size. In urban locations, on-street parking which is located either in front of or in close proximity to the front door of your business is highly desirable.

Unfortunately, too many business owners think that front door parking is reserved for them. This situation becomes intolerable if employees also park in front of or as close to the front door as possible. Owners are advised to require that all of their part-time and full-time employees park well away from the front door. In addition, they need to hold themselves to this same high standard. If owners and employees want to park near a door then they need to get used to parking at the rear door of a business.

**Grid Streets.** This is a very desirable type of street system because it provides added convenience for your customers. Grid streets are synonymous with interconnecting streets—something which enable customers to get to and leave your place of business more quickly. Unfortunately, in most suburbs, especially in newer suburbs, this kind of street system is largely absent. On the other hand, grid streets are much more common in urban areas and in older suburban communities.

**Growth Indicators.** In order to gauge the dynamics of an area, you need to look beyond factors such as traffic counts, anchors, rents, and vacancies. You need to learn about important growth indicators such as new postal drops, new building permits, new housing starts, recently approved subdivision plats, projected increases in school enrollment, and, new residential, commercial, industrial, educational, and institutional construction activity. Without knowing about what's planned for the future of an area how can you justify making a significant financial investment?

**Gut.** This one word describes the popular decision-making process used by far too many people when it comes to site selection. Remember, picking "home run" locations is a lot more about science than art—a message which is often ignored.

**Highest & Best Use.** This is a favorite term of real estate appraisers, bankers, developers, and city planners. It refers to land uses and focuses on which uses are most appropriate for a particular area. In many instances, most appropriate refers not so much to land use compatibility as to tax base enhancement. In most highway interchange areas and most commercial corridors, highest and best use means that retail, restaurants, gas, banks, motels, and offices are preferred land uses.

**Hole in the Fabric.** This terminology refers to the importance of finding a site which is located within a business cluster—one which enjoys a continuous flow of customer traffic as opposed to one which is characterized by either leapfrog development or incompatible neighboring uses.

While especially important to businesses which rely primarily upon pedestrian traffic, determining whether a hole in the fabric exists is absolutely essential when considering sites which are totally dependent upon vehicular traffic. In the case of the latter, simply being located five hundred or one thousand feet away from a neighboring business may make the difference between staying open or closing your doors.

**Hours of Operation.** This important factor can easily be overlooked when evaluating sites for your business. For all but a handful of businesses, you want to locate in an area where your planned hours of operation are similar to the majority of other nearby businesses. If you are looking to maximize customer traffic until 9:00 pm and find that most of your neighbors and most nearby businesses are not open past 6:00 pm, then you are going to be disappointed unless you operate a destination type business.

**Image.** Not only does your place of business need to project curb appeal, it needs to make a positive impression from the moment someone walks through the front door. This means that, in addition to attractive signing, inviting windows and convenient parking, your business needs to be bright, clean and well laid out. Furthermore, customer service needs to be courteous, friendly, and helpful. Remember that a customer's image of your business is what helps drive sales.

**Income Levels.** In order to avoid expensive mistakes, it is important to match the income levels in either a new or potential trade area with those which have been previously identified in your customer profile. An upscale restaurant or retail store, for instance, should concentrate its site selection efforts primarily in areas with many moderate and upper income households.

**Infrastructure.** Besides streets, the availability of sewer, water and gas are absolute prerequisites for retail and restaurant development. Two other improvements which can have a significant impact on boosting future sales are the number of curb cuts serving a site and the proximity of traffic signals.

**Lighting.** Having high levels of both storefront and parking lot lighting is an absolute must, especially if your retail store or restaurant hopes to attract significant numbers of women. Out of a concern for personal safety, women will not make site visits to businesses which are not well lit.

**Lower Level Space.** This type of space has a real visibility problem. Like basement space, it should be avoided unless money is no object and failure is an acceptable risk. The only time such "stigmatized" space might be justified is if your business is highly specialized and is, in fact, a true destination.

**Neighboring Land Uses.** By all means, pay attention to which types of land use are located either next to or very close to your business. Certain types of land uses are not compatible and can have a negative impact on both your customer traffic and sales. Especially unappealing neighbors are vacant parcels of property and businesses which generate loud noises, odors, and what could be construed to be the wrong type of customer.

**Number of Traffic Lanes.** The best locations for retail and restaurant businesses are those with one or two lanes of traffic moving in either direction. Traffic arteries with more than three to four lanes in either direction may end up discouraging, as opposed to encouraging, business patronage. In many instances less is more.

**Observations.** There is no substitute for not only making but recording personal observations. Simply visiting a site and leaving impressed is not enough. Indeed, evaluation is an absolute must. Stated differently, it is the name of the game.

**On-Street Parking.** Being able to provide customers with conveniently situated on-street parking, regardless of whether it is angled or parallel, is highly desirable. While free on-street parking is much more preferable than metered on-street parking, the latter is ok if it allows people to park for more than fifteen minutes, and, if it is reasonably priced. Nothing chases away existing or potential customers faster than being issued a parking ticket.

**One Way Streets.** Communities of all sizes contain one way streets in certain sections of their business districts. They are not, however, highly desirable from either a customer convenience or customer intercept perspective. In addition, they appear less pedestrian friendly to people than two way streets, in part because they encourage not only lane changes but higher speeds.

**Outdoor Seating.** This amenity is increasingly becoming a visible feature in both shopping centers and lifestyle centers. In particular, many casual and quick service restaurants are beginning to require that outdoor seating be incorporated into the design of their lease space.

This is an especially important amenity during warm weather months—one which provides a definite boost to business. Outdoor seating, whether at a table or bench, enables people to relax outdoors while indulging in a favorite pastime: people watching. Similarly, it provides customers with the opportunity to be entertained by everything that is happening around them. In short, it revels in being a happy place.

Outdoor seating also provides another notable benefit, something which is absolutely priceless—free advertising. However, you need to be very careful about the placement of outdoor seating. Because sitting in the hot afternoon or evening sun can be uncomfortable, you need to make sure that no patio, deck, courtyard, plaza, or sidewalk seating faces either west or south. Rather, unless shaded by canopies, umbrella, trees, or a building, only east and north facing seating is recommended.

**Parking Garages.** Both parking lot and on street parking are preferred alternatives to garage parking. However, parking garages, especially those located in downtown and regional mall areas, are a viable option for providing conveniently situated customer parking. The primary drawbacks of structured parking are their cost, the perception that they may be unsafe, and the potential to forget where you parked.

**Parking Lots.** Surface parking lots have become ubiquitous. To the dismay of many, they are asphalt jungles—places which are uninviting because they typically are devoid of humanizing amenities such as landscaping, crosswalks, and trees.

Whether located in the front, back and/or side of a building, large parking lots can turn out to be hot, poorly maintained, and potentially unsafe places to be. Yet, there is no denying that they provide convenient retail and restaurant customer parking opportunities and will continue to be an essential element of the local landscape.

**Parking Ratio.** In suburban settings it is especially important to understand how much parking your business requires. If you are already in business you should have a pretty good idea of how many parking spaces are needed, not just for customers but also for employees. If you are starting up a business or are moving to a different type of location then you should spend some time checking out how many parking spaces your competitors provide.

In no instance should you rely solely on zoning requirements, in part because they are often stated as minimum requirements. Retail uses, depending on size, will almost always require fewer parking spaces than restaurants. Generally speaking, retail and restaurant businesses will require anywhere from five to twenty parking spaces per one thousand square feet of floor area.

Remember that insufficient parking could have a negative impact on customer sales. Indeed, without adequate on-site or off-site parking you not only are guilty of gambling but risk staying in business.

**Primary Streets.** These streets comprise a network of well known travel arteries in every community. They not only carry high volumes of vehicular traffic but are typically associated with congestion, numerous and frequent curb cuts, and lots of traffic signals. Still, they are where most businesses want to locate.

**Sales Transfer.** See Cannibalization.

**Sidewalks.** While every business, large or small, will benefit from having sidewalks, not every property features this kind of amenity. Sidewalks provide an important means of helping link businesses and customers, especially in pedestrian friendly areas such as downtowns and neighborhood business districts. Sidewalks can be covered or open to the sky—each has its advantages and disadvantages. Typically, the wider a sidewalk is in front of a business the more inviting it becomes not only for customer traffic, but for outdoor display and seating purposes.

**Site Model.** Anyone who is involved in site selection needs to have a model or a system in place in order to standardize and subsequently guide his or her site search, analysis, and conclusions. Unfortunately, very few small businesspeople embrace this approach. Instead, too many small businesspeople employ a "seat of the pants" (hit and miss) approach which relies too heavily on two subjective variables: gut and emotion. It is this kind of hands off approach which helps to explain why so many new businesses fail within a relatively short time.

**Site Selection Scorecard.** This is a simple tool for evaluating whether or not a site grades out as an A, B, or C location. An example of such a scorecard is included in Chapter Seven.

**Slope.** See Site Grade in Chapter Two.

**Standards.** In order to start your quest for a "home run" location you need to establish quantifiable standards. **How many** parking spaces will your business require? **How much** store frontage do you need? **How much** window space do you need? **How many** square feet do you need to either lease or buy? **How large** does your outdoor patio need to be? **How many** signs can you display on the property? **How much** traffic passes by your front door every day?

The answers to these and other similar questions will enable you to not only determine whether the minimum site selection standards you have identified have been met, but, permit you to begin comparing sites. Accordingly, you will be able to measure how Site A stacks up against other sites.

Without identifying standards prior to beginning your site search efforts, you are not only "rolling the dice" but you are charting a course to fail—something which, with a little bit of homework, is very preventable!

**Surveys.** See Customer Interviews in Chapter Five.

**System for Success.** Securing the right location will not, by itself, be enough to make your business a success story. This may surprise you. However, the right location is only one of many, many factors which will influence how successful your retail or restaurant operation becomes.

What you need to understand as early in the business cycle as possible is that **you need a system for success.** This is one of the reasons why buying a franchise is attractive to so many start-up businesspeople. While by no means an automatic guarantee for success, by investing in a franchise which has a track record—meaning that it has been in business for several years and has multiple locations—you are investing in an entity which has established a formula for success.

A system for success, at a minimum, includes not only having a good location, but a strong drive to succeed and being either a good or a great operator. If you don't have these three building blocks you won't be able to create a strong foundation for future business success.

**Target Customer. If you don't know who your target customer is then you shouldn't be in business.** Yet, the sad truth is that way too many small businesses have absolutely "no clue" about who their best customers are.

Your target customer group will consist of your best customers—the ones who patronize your business the most often. While eighty percent of your business will likely not come from only twenty percent of your customers the lesson to be learned is that your repeat customers are the ones who you need to focus your efforts on. Repeat customers are also the one group who should be at the top of your marketing contact list.

If you are already in business and you want to learn who your target customers are then **you are strongly advised to periodically conduct customer surveys**. Doing so, along with demographic and psychographic data collection, will provide you with lots of reliable information and permit you to create a profile of your target customers.

If you do not currently operate your own business, then you need to understand as much as possible about the customer profile of your competitors. This is not an easy task, but is something which starts with your becoming a customer of your competition and making as many observations as possible. Also, don't be afraid to speak with the hired help. Without realizing it, they can often be a "gold mine" of useful information.

**Traffic Count.** Knowing how many vehicles pass by your site each and every day is important. While lots of traffic may lead to periodic traffic congestion, it is certainly preferable to having only a small amount of vehicular traffic pass by your front door on a daily basis.

This important information is usually available at city and county offices as well as at your state department of transportation office. In addition, planning organizations represent another good source for such information. Recorded traffic counts may or may not be up to date. However, they will usually be fairly current and will allow you to compare two or more locations.

**Tenant Mix.** If you are considering opening your business in a shopping center one of the first things you should consider is the type of tenant mix that exists. Are there tenants whose business is compatible with your business? Are there tenants who are likely to attract the same types of customers as your business? Is the mix of tenants likely to increase the number of people walking through your front door? Is there an anchor tenant who will not only provide an immediate identity for the shopping center but generate a significant amount of customer traffic? Are there tenants whose customers will compete with your customers for convenient parking opportunities?

**Traffic Generators.** Unless your business is either a convenience or destination business, one which will attract customers regardless of how many other retail stores and restaurants are located nearby, you should strive to be in the same general area as one or more major traffic generators. Examples include malls, lifestyle centers, big box stores, cinemas, restaurants, grocery and drugstores, office buildings, hospitals, schools, hotels, recreation complexes and industrial parks.

**Traffic Stacking.** While regulated by zoning and typically associated with congestion, traffic stacking needs to be considered if you are the owner or the operator of a restaurant which features an order (menu) board and a drive thru window. Being able to safely stack multiple vehicles one after another is very important. Perhaps even more important, however, is the ability to quickly move each vehicle through the line. Ideally, the best way to prevent unnecessary traffic stacking is to create a bypass lane. These approximately twelve foot wide lanes enable vehicles to either get out of line or continue driving around a building without becoming stuck in line.

**View Corridors.** All too often, developers and property owners permit buildings to be built on outlots in front of their shopping centers. While one or more outlots will maximize visibility for their end users, they typically end up blocking visibility for businesses which are located behind them. This is a preventable problem.

If zoning doesn't require that a good sized view corridor, typically two hundred front feet or more, be maintained between buildings, then developers and property owners are advised to adopt such a standard. The open areas which separate outlot buildings are ideally suited for parking, outdoor dining, and landscaping. If not excessively landscaped with trees, especially evergreen trees, these open areas can provide the types of view corridors which will insure that the identification signs of individual shopping center tenants will remain visible from the street.

If visibility becomes a problem for one or more shopping center tenants their business will suffer, tenant turnover will occur, vacancies will increase, rents will decrease, and property values will decline. Furthermore, once customer traffic at a shopping center begins to decline, typically what happens next is that outlot users will also experience a reduction in customer traffic. Thus, by simply maximizing the extent of view corridors a vicious cycle of decline can be prevented.

**View Time.** When you are driving, your rate of speed will determine how long you see a building or a sign. The faster you are driving the less opportunity you will have to read names and make out details. Conversely, the lower your speed the greater the opportunity you will have to make out names and details. For most businesses, being visible for just four or five seconds is sufficient time for name recognition to occur.

**Voids Analysis.** This is an exercise which many businesspeople conduct. Where voids exist, they often explain why people elect to open their businesses where they do. While conducting a voids analysis is a good starting point it is just that—it should not prevent you from doing additional homework.

As you should be aware from reading the contents of this guidebook, making "smart" location and "smart" site selection decisions is not easy. It is not only time consuming, but is absolutely essential to being able to secure "home run" locations.

**Windshield Survey.** Also known as drive bys, this is a good way to scout retail and restaurant properties. By using the PASTA V method which is described in detail in Chapter One you can quickly determine whether a property merits further evaluation or should be eliminated from your site search.

**Zip Codes.** Many big box businesses regularly track customers by zip codes—something which is ok if your trade area extends beyond three miles and ten minutes. However, for those businesses whose customers either live or work within one to two miles and are coming from three to five to seven minutes away, relying primarily on zip code information to begin building a customer profile is not recommended. From a comparability perspective, one reason for not being overly dependent on zip code information is that zip codes encompass a variety of both geographic sizes and population totals—from large to small. In addition, they are likely to contain only a fraction of the customers who frequent your business.

Zip code research can, however, serve as an invaluable introduction to the different types of population groups residing within a particular area. Such research allows you to quickly gain an understanding of where your customers live.

When I look at zip codes, I focus my efforts on learning about a select group of variables. For instance, if I'm working on behalf of a premium ice cream company, I want to quickly educate myself about median income levels, housing values, the percentage of people working in professional capacities, and the percentage of people with college degrees. Doing this kind of research enables me to almost effortlessly understand where I need to initiate both my location and my site selection efforts.

**Zoning.** Every urban and suburban community is likely to have adopted zoning regulations in order to control land uses, parking, signing, building setbacks, and much, much more. As such, one of the first things you need to do when conducting your site evaluation is to identify its zoning classification.

While many businesses are classified as Principal Permitted Uses, others may be classified as Conditional Uses. If your business falls into the latter category, chances are that you will need to secure permission from a local Planning and/or Zoning Commission rather than from administrative staff. In such instances, be prepared to live with one or more restrictive conditions.

Site plan requirements are another familiar provision of local zoning codes. While mostly associated with new development, they are likely to also apply to businesses intending to either occupy or expand existing space. This is where you may need to employ the services of a local architect or engineer.

Signing is heavily regulated. From window to building facade signing to multi-tenant and/or monument signing you need to check with either local zoning officials or an experienced sign company in order to make absolutely sure that your proposed signing complies with adopted requirements.

In certain instances, zoning restrictions will govern business hours of operation, especially in areas where nearby rooftops exist. In other instances zoning will require the provision of landscape buffers, trash enclosures, and parking lot lighting. Even outdoor seating is likely to be governed by zoning.

Many retail, restaurant, and shopping center properties are designed to satisfy minimum zoning requirements—something which can be a huge mistake, especially with respect to businesses which need higher levels of parking.

Typically, five parking spaces per one thousand square feet of building space is a common zoning standard. While this may be ok for most retail uses it can prove to be completely inadequate for restaurants, sports bars, pubs, and taverns. These are uses where both the number of seats and the number of employees need to be factored into the equation. As such, required parking will more closely resemble fifteen to twenty spaces per one thousand square feet.

Before you sign an agreement to either purchase or lease property please make sure that you visit or call local zoning officials. Doing so will not only be informative but will end up being time well spent.

# Chapter Four

## Selecting The Type of Location Which Best Suits Your Business

**Airport Locations.** Catering strictly to the convenience needs of passengers the only kinds of businesses with a history of succeeding in airports are those selling food, drinks, and convenience items, magazines, books, and newspapers. Here, small ticket items which are sold by large vendors with a nationwide reach are the norm.

Like other business areas, airports have "home run" locations as well as their fair share of lesser performing locations. Finding traditional or kiosk space in a busy central as opposed to modestly trafficked edge location will cost you more but is your best bet for driving higher sales volumes and generating higher profits.

If you are a local merchant with a specialty food product, you are advised to not only consider airport space which is located in a business cluster, but, only in one that isn't so large that your business will be in danger of getting lost in the crowd. Here, you are looking to join a group of businesses which benefit not only from good name recognition, but also collectively feature a variety of purchase choices.

When making your evaluation don't be shy about talking to the managers of businesses which are located within the business cluster you are considering. In addition, be prepared to observe as well as record customer traffic levels during both weekday and weekend peak periods.

The advantage of renting space in a business cluster is that it will enable you to benefit from the significant customer traffic that the more well known businesses generate—something which will initially help you build customer visits. From there, how good an operator you are will end up determining whether your business succeeds or fails.

**College & University Locations.** While these types of locations feature a "captive" student audience you need to understand that the great majority of them are on campus for only about nine months a year. As such, your business will experience peaks and valleys with respect to annual sales.

With few exceptions, college and university locations are all about convenience. For fast food (quick service) restaurants, locating either on campus in a food court, or, on the "main drag" is very important. In the case of the former you can expect your business to occur primarily over a two hour (11:30 am to 1:30 pm) lunch period. No such limitation exists, however, for off campus restaurants.

Ideally, you should strive to find a location which is in the heart of a commercial strip rather than on its edge. Also, don't lose sight of the fact that being located just one block off the "main drag" can mean that a substantial amount of student traffic will likely be intercepted by your competition before it ever makes it inside your front door.

Pizza and sub sandwiches are by far the two most popular types of food that college students consume on a regular basis. If you are in a different type of restaurant business then locating either near or in a cluster of pizza and sub restaurants will help you gain valuable exposure as well as increase customer sales.

While there is definitely a place for retail stores near college and university campuses they represent a higher risk than restaurants, in part because they are much more of a luxury rather than a necessity. As such, you will need to spend more money marketing your business if you are going to build name recognition and attract customers from non campus neighborhoods.

**Community Shopping Center Locations.** These are relatively large shopping centers consisting of approximately 150,000 square feet on about 15 or so acres. They are typically anchored by retail clothing stores and one or more small box stores. In certain instances, name brand bookstores will also be represented. While not as common today as in the past, grocery stores continue to serve as anchors for many community shopping centers.

Community shopping centers are major traffic generators. However, they can be challenging locations for small businesses to succeed in. This is partly due to the fact that buildings are typically located a good distance from the street, individualized storefronts and small spaces are almost never the norm, and, conveniently situated customer parking is almost always at a premium.

**Convenience Locations.** Convenience is, indeed, king. Increasingly, time or lack of it, is becoming a major influence in determining how we make our shopping and eating decisions. Every minute is valuable, especially during busy periods like the morning rush hour and the proverbial lunch hour.

Convenience locations are not always characterized by a convenience store or a gas station. Indeed, today convenience locations are just as likely to consist of freestanding banks, coffee shops, and fast food (quick service) restaurants.

Being able to easily get in and out of a business location is absolutely essential to not only attracting customers but to boosting sales. If your observations reveal that finding a parking space is a problem or that traffic stacking leads to congestion then the smartest thing you can do is to extend your site selection search.

**Convenience Shopping Center Locations.** Convenience shopping centers represent a great opportunity for the small business community. Typically small in size—they generally consist of approximately 10,000 to 15,000 square feet—they are built close to the street in order to maximize visibility, feature easy ingress and egress, offer lots of front door parking, and promote synergy between two or more businesses.

The negatives associated with convenience shopping centers are that they are typically unanchored and typically do not offer a lot of extra parking. For someone in the restaurant business a lack of sufficient parking should be a warning sign—don't take the risk.

**Corner Lot Locations.** This type of property is always in high demand—especially when convenience is a primary site selection criteria. Because corner locations are typically expensive to acquire they need to generate high sales volumes.

Corner locations provide businesses with enhanced visibility, parking, and signing opportunities. In addition, they are typically characterized by an increased number of curb cuts as well as higher traffic counts. Collectively, these factors help explain why corner locations are coveted by banks, coffee shops, convenience stores, gas stations, and quick service (fast food) restaurants.

If you have the resources to purchase a corner lot, you are advised to focus your efforts on acquiring a far corner. Look for sites which are served by traffic signalization. Avoid locations which sit opposite a median and be careful about committing to sites which are impacted by traffic stacking—something which can not only inhibit safe and convenient customer ingress and egress but harm future sales.

**Corner Space Locations.** Besides added exposure, the major benefit of these types of locations is the opportunity to feature glass wrap. If you are in the retail or restaurant business, having additional window area is very desirable, whether for customer seating or for merchandise display purposes.

Corner space locations also provide another important advantage: the opportunity for additional signing. Furthermore, such locations can provide opportunities for outdoor dining as well as for additional customer parking.

While corner locations will cost more, they are also likely to produce higher sales. As such, consider yourself fortunate if you find a good corner location.

**Crossroads Locations.** Similar to locating your business at a major street intersection, opening your business in an area where two major highways or roads meet can be a real positive. In both instances your business will benefit from not only increased traffic, but also increased exposure.

**Dense Urban and Dense Neighborhood Locations.** Every big city exhibits these types of locations. One way to differentiate dense urban and dense neighborhood locations from other types of business locations is their strong reliance on high levels of pedestrian rather than automobile traffic to generate sales. These types of locations, however, can present a major challenge: how does your retail store or restaurant stand out in a crowd? How can it not only differentiate itself from adjoining and nearby businesses but become memorable?

Dense urban and dense neighborhood locations can create a unique identity for themselves by doing one or more of the following: create a recessed entryway, use a variety of colors, incorporate a variety of building materials, and, make use of window awnings and entry canopies.

Other ways to stand out include: install one or more bay windows, add sidewalk and/or patio seating, display one or more flower boxes, use projecting signing, add banners and/or flags, and, like Google, use two or more colors in your name.

More ways to distinguish your business include: feature neon window signs, provide special lighting, use symbols to heighten sign awareness, display an oversized or colorful clock, show the current temperature, and add a window television—especially if it provides sports scores or stock market pricing.

Several other means of distinguishing your place of business include: framing your sidewalk with brick or creating a paver pattern, display an attention getting mannequin or statue, add gooseneck building lighting, play music, make use of building columns, and feature clever window signing like "Free Smells."

Businesses wishing to locate in dense urban and dense neighborhood locations should emphasize being within easy walking distance of one or more major traffic generators such as offices, retail anchor and specialty stores, hotels, restaurants, major tourist attractions, train and/or subway stations, performing arts centers, large parks, open space facilities like plazas and squares, and rooftops. Securing a location which relies on more than one of these types of land uses to generate customer traffic is highly desirable.

Finding space in an area with some immediate or nearby on street parking should be regarded as a bonus. In addition to locating your business in a busy, safe, and well lit area, being able to secure a site which is characterized by lots of pedestrian traffic throughout both the daytime and evening hours should be a high priority.

**Downtown Locations.** Years and years ago, every city's downtown was the place for retail and restaurants to be. However, due to the expansion of suburban malls and the introduction of power centers and lifestyle centers, downtowns have, for the most part, become substantially less attractive places to operate a business, especially a retail business.

Cities have increasingly been willing to diversify their business mix beyond offices, hotels, retail and restaurants. By relying upon programming as well as one of a kind uses such as convention centers, performing arts centers, libraries, museums, cinemas, theatres, plazas and squares, sports facilities, and new rooftops, cities have been able to attract more people downtown more frequently and for lengthier periods of time.

While downtowns are full of B and C locations they don't offer as much in the way of A locations. Therefore, you want to focus your site search efforts on locations with lots of slow moving traffic and lots of pedestrian activity—preferably areas where other retail stores and restaurants are clustered and where other nearby major traffic generators are located. Being near or in close proximity to major transportation hubs, large concentrations of parking, and lots of employment are recommended.

You are further advised to concentrate your site search in areas which are in the center of activity as opposed to being located on the edge of the central business district. In addition, be careful that you don't underestimate the importance of good nighttime lighting and areas which are perceived as being not only safe but clean. Furthermore, if you want to maximize customer opportunities always prioritize street level as opposed to second floor or lower level space.

**End Cap Locations.** Businesses which occupy the end (corner) space in a building are not only more visible, but offer a number of other advantages. These range from increased signing opportunities to the potential for not only more parking, but more convenient parking, increased window area, outdoor seating, and increased landscaping.

In the site selection hierarchy of location options end caps are more desirable than in line locations. They are in much demand by anchor tenants. However, they are a less attractive option than freestanding buildings. Drugstores are a great example of businesses which have previously occupied lots of end cap locations and have subsequently transitioned into freestanding buildings. In the process, they added prescription pick up windows which have enabled them to generate higher sales levels.

**Factory Outlet Locations.** Outside of an occasional small food court space, very few start-up and/or small business owners will ever have the opportunity to locate in these types of interstate highway and vacation dependent destination focused locations. This is the domain of mostly national chain stores. Even without a major anchor store factory outlet locations have become very popular. They attract not only residents living within an approximately one hour drive but travelers and even buses filled with tourists.

**Food Cluster Locations.** Food clusters are wonderful for not only creating synergy among various businesses but for creating unique destinations which have a significant amount of drawing power. Here the emphasis is on choice—a factor which helps to explain their popularity.

Businesses which are in a food cluster needn't be located side by side like you would expect to find in a mall food court. Rather, they can be concentrated in a particular area or along a particular street. While some businesses may end up competing with one another, for the most part they actually end up expanding business for one another.

Food clusters bring to mind the old saying "where there's smoke there's fire." When scouting for locations they should definitely be on your radar screen.

**Food Court Locations.** Malls have long known how to create activity. Mall food courts are one of their success stories. Food courts create the ultimate convenience, not only for people visiting a mall but also for the hundreds of employees who work there on a daily basis.

While rents can be high and the hours can be demanding, food court locations are a great place for national, regional, and sometimes local businesses to rent space. While finding a seat can be a slight negative it is also a wonderful testimonial to the popularity of food courts. The synergy and choices which food courts provide are also significant and serve as a model for developers and landlords in other types of venues such as factory outlet centers and lifestyle centers.

**Freestanding Building Locations.** In many instances the ultimate retail and/ or restaurant location is one which features a freestanding building. Coupled with good visibility, good ingress and egress, good signing, and sufficient parking, freestanding buildings have advantages that end cap and in line locations don't.

Freestanding buildings are typically more expensive to own and rent than either end cap or in line locations. However, the extra costs associated with occupying such buildings can be justified by the fact that, in most instances, they will generate higher sales levels. In the long run, spending a little extra money in order to provide your business with a freestanding building address should end up being a wise investment.

**Highway Interchange Locations.** While not always welcomed by local residents, highway interchanges have become ubiquitous across the United States. In particular, they have become popular locations for fast food (quick service) restaurants, the sale of gas and convenience items, and motels. Busy highway interchange locations generate customer traffic morning, noon, and night.

If you are in the restaurant business you want to be as close as possible to gas stations. Similarly, if you are in the gas business you want to be next to or near restaurants. Together, these two types of land uses illustrate the power of synergy to boost customer traffic and sales.

If you are contemplating opening a business at a highway interchange location, be careful not to locate too far from one or more of the area's major traffic generators. Nevertheless, don't be fooled into thinking that you can sacrifice any of the six keys which are described in Chapter One and end up being successful. Unfortunately, this is a mistake that too many small businesspeople who are in a hurry to open their doors make.

**Icon Locations.** If you look hard and long enough you will find an icon location. These are older, sometimes historic places which are special, either from a design standpoint or from the feeling you get from being there. In this case "there" can mean a street, an area, or a business district.

Icon locations are high profile locations. They typically have lots of eye appeal. Because they project a positive image they tend to be in strong demand. Icon locations establish the impression that what a particular business represents and what they are selling is something special, something unique, something which may even be one of a kind.

It is not uncommon for national retail and restaurant companies to seek out iconic building locations in iconic areas and/or in iconic business districts because they are the types of locations which help them differentiate themselves from their competitors. Starbucks is a good example of a company which likes to rent space in icon locations.

**Industrial Park Locations.** With few exceptions, industrial parks are hard pressed to generate a great amount of retail and/or restaurant business given the limited amount of daily traffic they generate. As such, businesses are better off locating on the perimeter or edge of such facilities. Here they are much more likely to serve customers coming from nearby rooftops, offices, retail, and/or motels.

**Infill Locations.** Land which remains undeveloped and properties which are ripe for redevelopment represent significant opportunities for accommodating new retail and restaurant projects in both older urban and suburban areas. While often expensive to acquire and time consuming to assemble they typically possess two very important building blocks for success: convenience to nearby rooftops and proximity to commercial critical mass.

In the future, interest in infill locations will become more prevalent, whether for small, medium, or large commercial and/or mixed use projects. If you have an interest in opening a business in such an area your best bet is to stay in touch with three parties: City Hall, area developers, and commercial realtors.

**In Line Locations.** Not every business wants or can afford a freestanding or an end cap location. Plenty of successful retail and restaurant businesses occupy in line space. The challenge for a new business is determining which in line space best meets their needs. In order to make not only an informed but a "smart" location and "smart" site selection decision the best thing you can do is to (a) look for a prominent building feature which differentiates your business from its neighbors and (b) incorporate one or more of the many ideas listed under the heading Dense Urban and Dense Neighborhood Locations into the design of your space.

**Intercept Locations.** Gas stations, banks, and convenience stores are examples of businesses which covet the types of locations where customers will think twice about driving past them in order to shop at a competitor location. The real key to consistently intercepting customer traffic is knowing which side of the street your business should be located on—the going to work side or the going home side.

**Interstate Locations.** The first two businesses that come to mind when the word interstate is mentioned are gas and food. Not only are they by far and away the two most popular land uses to be found at or near interstate highway interchanges, but two highly synergistic uses. If you didn't already know, McDonald's absolutely loves being next to gas and vice versa.

Highway interchange locations differ significantly from one place to the next and, by themselves, are no guarantee of success. If you are considering opening up a business at or near a highway interchange the first thing that you want to do is find out daily traffic counts. High is good. Low is bad. The second thing you want to do is measure critical mass. More is better. Like food and gas, traffic counts and critical mass are highly correlated.

One word of caution: don't expect to benefit from a highway interchange presence unless you are no more than twelve hundred to fifteen hundred feet or so from an exit ramp. Otherwise, the strong likelihood exists that your competition will end up intercepting potential customers and your business will likely lose out on potential sales. On the other hand, don't make the mistake of picking a site which, because it is closer to the interstate, suffers from such stumbling blocks as a lack of visibility and/or poor ingress and egress.

**Lifestyle Center Locations.** Lifestyle centers are the new focus for retail and casual dining restaurant activity. While not always anchored by a department store or one or more big box stores they are definitely attracting not only a lot of interest from businesses but high volumes of customer traffic.

Lifestyle centers are like all other shopping centers—they offer a variety of location types to prospective businesses. However, the simple truth of the matter is that some locations are destined to be better than other locations. In other words, not all lifestyle center locations have the potential to become "home run" locations.

All things being equal, the best locations in lifestyle centers are likely to be those which enjoy outstanding visibility, have one or more anchors as well as lots of parking nearby, and are located in areas with lots of pedestrian traffic.

**Lower Level Space Locations.** About the only thing that needs to be said for these types of locations is that you should avoid them.

**Main & Main Locations.** When two major streets or highways intersect you can typically expect to find a small, medium, or large cluster of retail and restaurant businesses. Such clustering is explained, in part, by the added convenience which major intersections provide and the increased traffic count and activity which they generate.

In addition to benefiting from heightened awareness, most urban as well as some older suburban Main & Main locations are characterized by another important advantage: they typically provide people with more than one means of access. In addition to being able to drive there, customers oftentimes have the choice of either being able to walk or take the bus. And, in certain high density communities, the ability to ride some form of rapid transit can play a major role in boosting customer counts.

Locating your business at or near a Main & Main location is something you should explore. Nonetheless, you need to make sure that sufficient customer parking exists, that neighboring businesses offer some level of synergy, that adequate signing exists, and that the demographics and psychographics in the immediate area match or have a high degree of correlation with your customer profile.

**Mixed Use Building Locations.** Mixed use buildings consist of a dominant use as well as one or more secondary business uses. In many instances, the dominant use will be either office or hotel and the secondary uses will consist of ground floor retail and/or restaurants. In certain instances, however, the dominant use will be residential condominiums and the secondary uses will be ground floor retail and/or restaurants.

Generating street-level customer traffic for a business which is located inside a low rise, mid rise, or high rise mixed use building can be tricky. Your immediate challenge will be to create a strong identity. Regardless of the amount of building frontage you have your best bet for maximizing storefront visibility is to feature the use of awnings—especially colorful awnings. Paired with memorable facade and window signing, awnings will help your business stand out.

A word of caution is in order. While some people may think that they have a built in or captive audience in the people who either live or work in a mixed use building you should not regard them as providing you with an abnormally high percentage of customers. Instead, your emphasis needs to be on attracting street level customer traffic. Such traffic will most likely account for the majority of your sales.

Given a choice, my preference for a dominant building use would be office, mostly because office workers represent the potential for generating morning, lunchtime, and after work retail and restaurant customer traffic. My secondary preference for a dominant building use would be residential as opposed to hotel.

All things being equal, I would not make locating a business in a building with a mix of uses a number one or top priority.

**Mixed Land Use Locations.** What I am referring to here is a mix of land uses as opposed to a mix of uses within a building. Besides offices and the three R's—residential, retail, and restaurant—mixed use locations typically feature a visitor lodging facility (hotel/motel), and/or an entertainment (cinema/theatre/museum) component. Here, cafes, bars, and pubs not only provide outdoor dining opportunities, but encourage people watching. A complimentary mix of retail stores is a bonus. Collectively, these elements can make mixed use locations vibrant, memorable, and special places to visit.

What the small business person should primarily be looking for in a mixed use location is a pedestrian friendly environment, a complimentary mix of uses, a high level of synergy between user types, and lots of curb appeal. Extended hours of operation beyond 8:00 or 9:00 pm can be a nice bonus. In addition, mixed use locations should also pass the PASTA V test. These influences can help prompt customer visits as well as sales.

**Neighborhood Locations.** There will always be strong demand for neighborhood retail and restaurant locations because of the unmatched convenience which they offer to nearby residents. Everyone has to go by them in order to patronize the competition. Some characteristics of neighborhood locations are: limited critical mass, little direct competition, affordable rents, and relatively small trade areas. These are the types of locations which foster more than their fair share of start-up as well as mom-and-pop businesses.

**Neighborhood Shopping Center Locations.** These are locations which typically have either a grocery or a drugstore as their anchor. Other businesses, from national chains to start-ups, like calling neighborhood shopping centers home.

Size wise, grocery and drugstore businesses are represented at the upper end of the square foot spectrum. Mid size businesses typically include a mix of table service restaurants, banks, and a variety of retail stores. At the small end of the scale you can expect to find pick up and delivery restaurants as well as service retail businesses such as bakeries, dry cleaners, florists, and nail salons. In most instances the owners of these types of small businesses are most frequently independent operators rather than chain operators. And typically the owners of businesses in neighborhood shopping centers live or have roots in either the nearby or surrounding area.

While neighborhood shopping center locations can be good or even excellent places to operate a business, it is paramount that local merchants not rely too heavily on grocery or drugstore anchors to generate high levels of customer traffic for them. Assuming that they will "dump" customers in your lap is not only unrealistic, but a dangerous approach to business.

If businesses in neighborhood shopping center locations really want to generate high square foot sales they need to first make sure that they satisfy all of the PASTA V location requirements which have been described in Chapter One. In addition to having either a good or superior location, small businesses need to offer superior quality as well as superior service. These benchmarks will not only help create to new customers, but will generate the best type of customers—the ones who choose to become repeat customers.

---

**Office Building Locations.** Opening either a retail store or a restaurant inside an office building not only limits your exposure, but also isolates you from other businesses. This, in turn, significantly reduces your ability to draw customer traffic from other areas. While having a monopoly is appealing, you can't afford to overlook the fact that you need to count on more than just office workers if you are going to maximize your sales.

**Office Park Locations.** Too many people think that locating their business in an office park is going to enable them to generate high sales volumes. Wrong! Like industrial parks, you want to consider sites which are located on the edge of an office park—locations which can take advantage of higher traffic counts and are more capable of capturing business from other nearby uses, especially nearby rooftops.

**Older Business District Locations.** Older business district locations, in part because of their affordable rents, are especially popular places for new start-up businesses. However, you need to be careful that adequate off-street parking exists not only for your customers but for your employees.

**One Hundred Percent (100%) Locations.** These are the "home run" locations that every company is looking for and wants to own or lease a lot of. For the small businessperson such locations are usually very difficult to secure because the cost of owning or renting them isn't cheap. Unfortunately, what I have learned over many years is that cheap is usually at the forefront of many small businesspeople's site selection criteria.

One hundred percent (100%) locations are worth their weight in gold. Not only do they pass the PASTA V test with flying colors, but, they end up consistently producing the kind of high customer traffic counts which result in outstanding profit opportunities. In the world of site selection it doesn't get any better than that.

**Outlot/Pad Locations.** Also known as pad sites, these locations offer excellent visibility from the street for either a single user, a co-branded building, or a small retail strip center with a limited number of tenants. They are a staple in front of larger shopping centers with one or more anchor tenants. Examples of such centers include regional malls, power centers, lifestyle centers, and discount centers.

Outlots may or may not have direct access to the street on which they are located but typically benefit from access to what is known as cross easement parking. While they aren't the cheapest places to own or rent, outlot locations are in great demand, primarily because the businesses which like to call them home generate sales which are consistently well above average.

**Park & Recreation Locations.** There are no businesses I know of that can be supported entirely by customer traffic either coming to or from a park and/ or recreation facility. Such facilities tend to not only be seasonal but cater primarily to impulse, small ticket purchases such as ice cream and beverages. If you own or operate a seasonal business, look for other nearby traffic generators, and, be very careful that you aren't the only business around.

**Pedestrian Friendly Business Locations.** Older business districts and older neighborhoods are typically pretty pedestrian friendly. This is because they weren't built to attract primarily customers who are almost exclusively dependent upon cars, SUVs, mini vans, and trucks to get around.

Pedestrian friendly locations are typically found in areas with moderate to high residential densities, a mix of surrounding or nearby land uses, few parking lots of any real size, wide sidewalks, blocks with few if any curb cuts, on-street parking opportunities, a network of nearby interconnecting streets, one lane of traffic moving in either direction, some form of mass transit, tree lined streets, and, streets with low posted speed limits.

Lifestyle centers are relatively recent examples of shopping center dominated developments which are designed to be more pedestrian friendly than almost all other types of shopping centers. They have been patterned after successful older business districts in order to create a more appealing and more vibrant pedestrian scene. In doing so they have captured the middle ground between yesterday's older areas and today's growing areas.

Pedestrian friendly business areas offer a trade off between customers who are walking and those who are driving to a particular destination or cluster of businesses. Ideally, a healthy mix of both will exist. In today's convenience dominated society, very few businesses can survive, let alone thrive, if they are dependent solely upon pedestrian traffic. Ironically, the availability of nearby parking opportunities, even if relatively limited, is absolutely essential to the success and longevity of the different types of businesses which are located in pedestrian friendly environments.

Large businesses such as grocery stores, modest size businesses such as drugstores, and smaller businesses such as fast food (quick service) restaurants are likely, for any number of reasons, to typically be absent from or avoid pedestrian friendly locations. Conversely, many types of small businesses fit easily into this once prevalent type of location. Bakeries, casual dining restaurants, specialty shops, sandwich shops, ice cream stores, jewelers, art galleries, frame shops, gift shops, florists, used bookstores, and coffee shops are some of the better known types of businesses which can commonly be found in pedestrian friendly locations.

**Plaza & Square Locations.** These are highly sought-after locations—that is if they are in the right area. Typically the right area means one which is pedestrian friendly, a location which not only welcomes but is capable of accommodating a crowd of people, and one which is surrounded by a synergistic mix of uses such as retail, restaurants, entertainment, offices, and hotels.

In all instances, some form of fixed seating is a major feature—an amenity which helps create the ideal place for people watching throughout much of the day and oftentimes late into the evening.

Plazas and squares are usually characterized by attractions such as a fountain, a grassy park, a staging or display area, and statuary. They are fun places to be, wonderful places to gather with friends and family or for events and special occasions.

Businesses serving food and drinks are good bets for locating either on or opposite plazas and squares. Restaurants, bars, coffee shops, and ice cream shops are just a few of the businesses which these types of special places frequently attract.

You can expect to pay a little more in rent for the privilege of opening a location in a plaza or square area. However, since you will be where the action is chances are extremely good that you can count on lots of people to walk by and hopefully stop into your business establishment.

**Power Center Locations.** Power centers are among the least pedestrian friendly of all shopping centers. Aesthetically, what is most memorable about them is a combination of blank walls, deep building setbacks, and underutilized parking lots.

Because they are the province of big and mid size box stores, the typical power center tenant mix is often devoid of small businesses. In such centers, the best locations for small businesses are out front on pads (outlots) where building and sign visibility can be maximized. Such locations enable a mix of freestanding retail and restaurant uses to intercept street traffic as well as cater to the customer traffic which either shops at or works in one or more power center stores.

**Regional Locations.** Regional locations are usually the first choice of national retail and restaurant chains—all of whom are interested in taking advantage of the surrounding area's critical mass as well as its anchor stores, synergy, connectivity, mix of uses, and high traffic counts. Another selling point is the fact that regional locations are usually at or near an interstate highway interchange—something which makes them very convenient to a whole lot of people.

**Regional Mall Locations.** Expensive but definitely worth considering is how I would classify such locations. Besides having the advantage of year-round temperature control, malls are bright, clean, interesting, and busy places to visit. Generally speaking, mall owners understand tenant mix and synergy better than other shopping center owners. They also understand marketing and programming better. As a result, the best regional malls typically generate some of the highest square foot sales in the shopping center industry.

Except for kiosk and seasonal operators, opportunities for local merchants to rent space in regional malls is typically pretty restricted. While retail and restaurant operators can expect to pay high rents here the beauty of a regional mall location is the unmatched guarantee of seven day a week year round traffic.

As is true of other shopping centers, remember that not all locations are created equal. Here you can find "home run" locations as well as average locations. While being close to anchor stores and food courts is typically high on every merchant's priority list don't overlook opportunities to be near synergistic uses—good neighbors can help to drive customer traffic to your store or restaurant.

**Street & Sidewalk Vendor Locations.** Most big cities have a variety of vendors who sell from street and sidewalk locations. Most of them are selling food. Others are there to sell jewelry and trinkets. All vendors need to be in high traffic locations in order to support their respective businesses. For the most part this means locating in front of or near downtown office buildings, retail clusters, convention centers, stadiums, and hotels.

Food trucks are the newest and fastest growing small business enterprise in many downtown areas. These vendors sell hot dogs, pizza, burritos, coffee, and other items—mostly during a relatively short period of time coinciding with people's lunch hours. Once seasonal, more and more food trucks are selling to consumers year round.

**Strip Locations.** Strip locations are ubiquitous across the United States. They are home to a vast array of fast food restaurants, convenience stores, gas stations, grocery and drugstores, all kinds and sizes of shopping centers, big box stores, motels, tire stores, auto parts stores, automobile dealers and the list goes on and on.

Mostly a result of the automobile friendly growth which took place in post World War II suburbs, strip locations can go for miles and miles. They are often laced with curb cut after curb cut, lots of traffic lights, telephone poles galore, uninspiring buildings, half empty parking lots, and sign after sign. Collectively, these characteristics help explain why some people consider strip locations to be, among other things, concentrations of urban blight.

Strip locations are characterized by high traffic counts—something which helps to explain their popularity. However, heavy traffic volumes and seemingly endless roadside clutter also contribute to the difficulty that many motorists experience when it comes to easily spotting individual retail and restaurant destinations. Therein lies the challenge for many small businesses—how to maximize visibility. Your location either has visibility or it doesn't—there is no in between.

Do you remember in Chapter One that visibility is listed as one of the six keys to site selection? If you want to stay in business the biggest favor you can do for yourself is to make sure that your sign(s) as well as your storefront or building have good visibility, not just from straight ahead (head on) but from a distance. The further away your business can be seen the better for you and your customers.

**Strip Shopping Center Locations.** Whether big, small, or medium in size, these are the most popular and numerous types of locations for local, regional, and national retail and restaurant companies.

It is important to remember that not all strip shopping centers are created equal. Some enjoy better visibility, more parking, and easier access than others. Similarly, some can point to more activity, higher traffic counts, and better signing than other nearby strip shopping centers. Your job is to determine which locations maximize your ability to generate sales.

Also, be aware of the fact that all locations within a strip shopping center are not created equal. End caps typically offer more glass, more parking, and more signing than in line space. This is one of the reasons they are favored by many restaurants and many retailers.

**Subway and Train Locations.** A number of big cities are served by subways and trains. This can result in people who live and work in the surrounding area periodically making trips back and forth to a subway or train station. These are people who are a good bet to make one or more convenience or impulse oriented purchases. They represent what is known in the business as "captive" audience sales.

Some transit oriented locations have heavy concentrations of office around them. Some are surrounded by a mix of residential types. Others may feature retail. In any case, a variety of retail and restaurant businesses are likely to be found either inside, next door to, or across the street from subway and train facilities.

Don't assume that your business can thrive solely off the customer traffic which is generated by subways and trains. Instead, think about the "capture rate"—what is the percentage of people who ride these alternative forms of transportation likely to spend money on either prior to boarding, or, upon exiting them? The answer typically is a fairly low percentage.

The most common types of businesses which are found either in or near subway and train stations include, in no particular order, bagel shops, carryout restaurants, coffee shops, convenience stores, fast food restaurants, liquor and tobacco stores, newsstands, and sandwich shops.

**Tourist Area Locations.** Because they tend to be seasonal, prospective businesspeople need to do lots of homework before locating in tourist areas. If you are considering renting or buying space in an urban tourist location you should look for a significant cluster as well as a good variety of businesses. A good example of a busy and very successful urban tourist attraction is Navy Pier in Chicago. It is a great model for attracting lots of people for lots of different reasons, not only during warm weather months, but year round.

Less urban locations can also be successful. However, without critical mass and a variety of synergistic attractions they are riskier places to make a major investment in, especially if they are located in an area where tourist traffic tends to be seasonal and is subject to large fluctuations of visitors. In these types of areas an emphasis needs to be placed on not only differentiating yourself from your competition but in selecting a site which is either in or near the heart of activity as opposed to being located on the edge of where all or the majority of tourist traffic is found.

**Truck Stop Locations.** Found at highway interchanges, newer truck stop locations offer a synergistic combination of gas, snack foods, beverages, and fast food. In almost every instance the names of the businesses who are located here are easily recognized, mostly national brands such as McDonald's, Subway, Wendy's, etc. Consequently, you will find very few mom-and-pop businesses at truck stop locations.

By themselves, truck stops are not much of an anchor. As such, other than convenience based businesses such as fast food (quick service) restaurants very few businesses are likely to benefit from the types and levels of traffic which truck stops generate.

**Upper Level Space**. Like lower level space, upper level space should be off limits unless the space you are considering is located in a vertical mall like Water Tower Place in Chicago.

About the only reason for justifying renting this kind of space is if you are in either the service retail or novelty retail business, and, you operate what can be classified as a destination business. For instance, a good beauty salon or a busy palates studio can succeed in upper level space if they are well signed, offer lots of natural light, and provide customers with an alternative means of access such as an elevator or an escalator.

In most situations the only three words you need to remember with respect to upper level locations are "no way, Jose."

# CHAPTER FIVE

## Other Important Site Selection Influences and Related Factors

**Advertising.** Does the shopping center you are located in or are thinking about leasing space in do any common advertising, especially with respect to informing people about how conveniently situated your business is to nearby anchor stores, major intersections, nearby cinemas, and/or area major traffic generators?

**Aerial Photographs.** Looking at aerial photos is a great way to become more familiar with the area surrounding the site you are considering. Pay special attention to proximity to anchor retailers and restaurants, site connectivity, and nearby competitors.

**Ambiance.** These are the things that make your business more memorable. Simple things like ceiling type, types and levels of lighting, flooring, wall coverings, decorative touches, booth and couch seating, a fireplace, and music can, individually or collectively, help create a positive and lasting impression. Examples of businesses who understand the intricacies of this important influence include Panera and Starbucks.

**Analog Model.** Initially developed by grocery store giant Kroger, this widely used system relies upon variables such as square footage, population, income levels, trade area size, site accessibility, traffic counts, critical mass, competition, and parking to forecast new store sales.

**Areas of Dominant Influence.** Just as each restaurant and retail store has its own customer trade area so does each metropolitan area. In the television, radio, and newspaper worlds they are better known as Areas of Dominant Influence (ADI).

Today, most franchisors look to Areas of Dominant Influence in order to determine the number of people who not only live in a particular area which they would like to have a presence in, but how many store or restaurant locations such areas can potentially support. As an example, a standard of one restaurant for every one hundred thousand people might be identified. It is this type of information which is then used as the basis for awarding area developer and franchisee territorial rights.

**Awnings.** A great way but often overlooked means of drawing attention to your store or restaurant is to use awnings. They come in many different colors and shapes, can be made out of a variety of materials, and, can easily accommodate the use of lettering, symbols, and lighting.

**Bay Windows.** The presence of bay windows is especially important whenever there is a limitation on the amount of natural light coming into your business, or, the need to create additional window display opportunities exists.

A secondary but important benefit of having one or more bay windows is that they help draw attention to your business. In this regard, they function a lot like awnings and signs.

**Benchmarks.** This is a comparative tool, something which enables you to evaluate how different sites stack up against one another. Primary factors such as total population, income levels, education levels, and housing values should be compared. In addition, other influences like traffic counts, critical mass, number of parking spaces, and the number and size of nearby anchors should be evaluated.

**Big, as in Building.** Is the space you rent or own or want to be in easily identified from the street or the parking lot, or does it somehow blend in and, as a result, get lost? For most retail and restaurant buildings small is better than big and few is better than more.

**Big, as in Space.** Most businesses don't need a whole lot of space. Indeed, if spaces were to be classified as being small, intermediate, and big, by far the largest number of retail stores and restaurants would be grouped into the former category while the least number of businesses would be grouped into the big category. A good way to remember this is to think of a pyramid.

**Board of Advisors.** Every big corporation in America has a Board of Directors. However, if you ask small business owners if they have a group of advisors who aren't involved in day-to-day operations and decisions the overwhelming answer will be no. A word of warning—this is not good business!

Don't think twice about asking your attorney, your accountant, your main supplier, your lender and/or your realtor to periodically meet as a group in order to help advise you on a variety of important matters. Their counsel will teach you a lot and cost you very little money.

**Brand Equity.** Name recognition is helpful and can be a powerful influence in building customer patronage. While this may not be a problem locally, the lack of brand equity in a new market can definitely inhibit store sales. While increasing your marketing budget can help build brand equity the best solution is to embark upon a program to open new "home run" locations and expand your market share.

**Brand Recognition.** Defining your business and differentiating it in the marketplace is what brand recognition is all about. As you embark upon expanding your business footprint you will find that brand recognition helps build customer awareness as well as customer patronage. And, it can generate not only more site and location opportunities, but also potential franchise opportunities.

**Build To Suit.** Periodically, retail and restaurant companies will look to one or more developers for build to suit opportunities. Instead of purchasing land, bidding the construction job, and building a new store or restaurant these businesses choose to contract with a developer in order to provide them with what amounts to a turn key building opportunity. Two of the major benefits of this type of development are that retail and restaurant businesses save both time and money. This enables them to not only open for business quicker but to realize a variety of cost savings—especially if they utilize the services of a preferred developer.

**Business Plan.** A business plan is essential for anyone who is contemplating going into business—especially if they are either going into business for themselves or will be applying for a bank loan. Business plans should not be done on a one time basis. Rather, they should be updated at least annually.

Among other things, a good business plan will clearly state your business objectives, list and describe start-up costs, identify your target customer, indicate how you plan to market your business, identify funding sources, spell out location specifics, and describe sales projections.

Business plans are one of the most overlooked tools for business success. If you want to learn more about business plans you should visit your local library or go to a good bookstore. Otherwise, browsing Amazon.com or conducting research via Google is recommended. An overlooked but tremendously helpful business plan educational contact is your local SCORE (Service Core of Retired Executives) chapter. You should definitely consider calling and scheduling an appointment with a counselor. It will be one of the best investments you ever make.

**Camera.** Whenever you visit a site or an area always have your camera with you so you can take a series of pictures. The human mind can only remember a limited amount of detail. Having pictures to study will definitely help you do a better job of evaluating the pros and cons of a site and its surrounding area.

**Census Tract.** This is a geographical area which the U.S. Census Bureau uses to gather a variety of household data. Census tracts serve as the basis for assembling important demographic information—something which, while only current for a short period of time, helps companies formulate their site selection criteria.

**Certified Site Selection Specialist.** Currently no such designation exits for professionals who assist small business owners and start-ups with site selection. This is an unfortunate oversight and needs to be corrected. Not everyone who is a commercial realtor is a site selection specialist. Indeed, most are not.

Just as the shopping center industry benefits from having Certified Shopping Managers and Certified Leasing Specialists so would the commercial real estate community if certification of site selection specialists were an option. In particular, more business owners and start-ups would recognize the benefit of working with a trained and highly skilled professional whose focus was on finding "home run" locations for his or her clients.

**Chambers of Commerce.** These are organizations which are pro business. They do a great job of promotion and have a membership roster which may become a valuable resource for not only data mining but business development. In many small communities Chambers of Commerce can be very helpful to the owners of start-up as well as existing retail and restaurant companies. However, in large cities and metropolitan areas where attracting large numbers of office and industrial jobs is a high priority these business organizations are much less of a resource.

**City Hall.** The planning, zoning, and economic development departments at City Hall should be one of your first stops when considering locations and site options. The public servants who work in these departments can provide you with answers to a wide variety of questions related to such things as permitted uses, curb cuts, parking requirements, permits, licenses, and signing. In addition, they can provide you with valuable statistical information.

**Comparative Analysis.** Never look at a site without comparing it to one or more additional sites. The same goes for comparing demographics, parking, signing, etc. This important exercise not only eliminates emotion and gut from the decision making process but helps businesspeople to differentiate great sites from good sites and good sites from average sites.

**Corridor Dynamics.** Ask yourself if the commercial area you are looking at is growing, stable, or beginning to decline? This is one of the first questions that needs to be answered. Areas which are characterized by business turnover, more than a little vacant land, bargain rents, empty storefronts, and aging properties are areas which present a "red flag." They are areas which present a high level of risk and should be avoided. The same advice applies to one dimensional areas and areas with little or no nearby housing.

**Co Tenancy.** This important term refers to a lease clause which can be very influential with respect to sustaining customer traffic and preventing a decline in your sales revenues. This is one instance where you are definitely advised to seek legal counsel.

The longevity and prosperity of one or more anchor or major tenants in the shopping center or building where your business is located is crucial to the longevity and prosperity of your business. As such, you want to make sure that if an anchor or major tenant leaves, otherwise known as going dark, or occupancy levels fall below a certain level, that you are entitled to some form of rent relief, or, are able to either scale back your hours of operation or break your lease.

**Covered Walkways.** These can be both a blessing and a curse. While they permit shopping center customers to walk or sit outside without any direct exposure to rain, snow, or the hot sun they can also make buildings and display windows look less inviting to customers—especially if they are either north or east facing.

**Creating A Memorable Experience.** Creating a memorable experience for your customers is important, especially in the restaurant business where being able to differentiate your business from your competitors is so important. Yet, creating a memorable experience is not only challenging but seldom achieved—the proverbial "easier said than done." You'll know it when you feel it is the best way to describe what a memorable experience is. That means feeling something special, something unique, something to cherish.

A hospitality attitude combined with factors such as memorable building and interior design, quality, selection, and the opportunity to observe (watch) other people are some but not all of the components which help to create a memorable experience—something all of us want more of. A great example of a company that understands the importance of creating a memorable experience better than just about any other company is Starbucks.

**Credit Scores and Financial Statements.** These constitute the litmus test for most landlords who lease space to small and start-up businesses. They are looking for high credit scores and financial statements which show that you have little debt and an attractive net worth. The combination of these important factors will automatically elevate not only landlord interest levels but your ability to negotiate better terms for yourself with respect to rent, build-out, and/or a tenant improvement allowance.

**Customer Address File.** This is relatively easy to accomplish if your business accepts checks, issues "loyalty" cards, does catering, and/or makes deliveries. With a little bit of effort it can also be used in conjunction with credit cards. Another way to capture this important information is to simply ask customers for their address.

Once this important information is available you will have established the basis for a market data base which can be used to stay in touch with customers via periodic mailings. In addition, it can provide you with a wonderful opportunity to create a spotting map which identifies where your customers live. This, in turn, will give you an excellent idea of the geographic reach (trade area) of your business.

**Customer Frequency.** Repeat customer business is much more important to your success than the business which is provided by the occasional or infrequent customer. This, unfortunately, is a little understood success dynamic.

Someone who spends money in your store or restaurant once a month as opposed to 2-3 times a year should be your target customer—the customer whom you want to continue doing business with on a regular basis.

**Customer Interviews.** Periodically talking with your customers is absolutely essential. Nonetheless, my experience reveals that very few businesses ever spend time doing such research. Whether face-to-face interviews or interviews over the telephone are conducted they are easy to do and can be relatively inexpensive.

Businesses who fail to conduct customer interviews forfeit a tremendous opportunity to learn as much as possible about their customers. Besides observing whether they are male or female and what their general age group is, you should ask questions which reveal where they live or work, whether they rent or own a home, their education and income levels, where else they shop or eat, how long it took them to get to your store or restaurant, and how many times a month they patronize your business.

The number of questions you ask is up to you and is dependent upon how much customer information you wish to obtain. Interviews can last from less than a minute to several minutes. They can be conducted either in person or over the telephone. They can be conducted by business owners, one or more employees, by local college students, or by market research organizations.

Afterwards, it will be important to not only tabulate, but thoroughly analyze the interview results. Once these important tasks are completed you will have a much better understanding of who your customers are. In addition, you will be able to use this kind of data in order to seek out other store or restaurant locations where similar types of customers are most likely to reside.

**Customer Lists.** Every small business should have an understanding of their customer base. In addition to individuals, you should know if certain groups, organizations, and/or other businesses help generate sales for your business. If so, they should be added to your customer address file and may even be a component of your customer interview effort.

**Customer Profile.** See Target Customer.

**Customer Relationships.** If you don't do a good job of establishing and maintaining customer relationships you won't be in business very long. Remember something very important: these are the people who pay for your car, your mortgage, your vacations, and your kids college educations. Ignore them and you are inviting trouble.

**Customer Service.** Most businesses get only one opportunity to make a positive first impression. Therefore, it is absolutely imperative that you train all of your employees on becoming customer focused, starting with a friendly greeting and a smile. Something so simple is, regrettably, one of the most overlooked opportunities for generating not only sales but repeat business.

High levels of customer service are absolutely essential for business success. If you are looking for a true competitive advantage your number one priority should be customer service. In the long run it could well turn out to be your holy grail!

**Customer Spotting Maps.** These are a critical but vastly underutilized resource tool for businesses of all kinds. Knowing where your customers originate their store or restaurant visits, whether from home, school, place of work, etc., is important information.

Customer spotting maps are easy to do. They can be completed by either asking customers questions or by having them locate, on a map, where their trip originated. This can be a fun exercise if you remember not to ask customers, especially females, for their home address—something many of them will be reluctant to reveal. Instead, ask them for the name of the street where they live, followed by the name of the closest intersecting street.

By using dots to indicate locations, you can easily develop a map which shows where your customers are coming from. This will enable you to define the geographic reach of your store or restaurant—otherwise known as your trade area.

**Customer Surveys.** Such surveys are distinguished from customer interviews primarily by the fact that they are not conducted in person. Rather, they are conducted through table top surveys, point of sale information, delivery records, a mailed survey instrument, or, an on line internet survey.

While these types of surveys can ask more questions than is typically the case in customer interviews whether a person chooses to respond or not is completely discretionary. Therein lies a potential problem because the universe of responses will shrink—sometimes considerably—in comparison with face-to-face interview opportunities. Thus, the reliability of customer surveys is diminished.

One of the best means of achieving survey "buy in" is to offer something to the respondent. For instance, an incentive might be the chance to be entered into a drawing for a prize. Another might be a gift certificate. Yet another might be to reward them with a small amount of money. If you aren't in a position to offer very much, then think about making a two-for-one offer, or, provide some type of discount, like fifty percent off.

**Daytime Businesses.** If your business is primarily a daytime business you want to pay special attention to who else in the immediate and nearby commercial area operates a daytime as opposed to an evening business. Why? Because the owners, managers, and employees of local businesses should be encouraged to become customers of your business. Similarly, you should become one of their customers. Such patronage will lead to something very positive—an increase in customer traffic for everyone.

**Daytime Visits.** When you are conducting your site search the best time to do so is intermittingly throughout a several day period of time for one or more weeks. A good rule of thumb to follow is to make an early morning, noontime, and late afternoon visit at least twice during the weekday and once over the weekend.

Every time you make a field trip be sure to spend the majority of your time on-site. However, don't neglect spending time making observations in the immediate and nearby commercial areas as well as in the surrounding residential areas. Otherwise, you won't be able to obtain a good understanding of the dynamics which are likely to impact potential store or restaurant revenues.

When you conduct each of your daytime visits you should plan on spending an hour or more making written observations, talking with people, and taking pictures. There is absolutely no substitute for doing this type of comprehensive research. Indeed, the more time you devote to making such trips the better prepared you will be to make a "smart" site selection decision.

**Desirability.** There is an old expression that "birds of a feather flock together." When conducting field research you should place an early emphasis on the desirability of not only the site you are considering but its general location. By way of example, if you are looking to cater to upscale customers you should only consider sites and areas which are attractive and appealing. To go into a less desirable setting is risky—very much a "role of the dice."

**Destination Uses.** This is a type of use which is the opposite of a convenience business. As an example, quick service (fast food) restaurants, unless highly specialized, draw people who either work or live in, or visit the nearby area. By contrast, casual dining and fine dining restaurants attract customers from a much larger area—one which instead of catering to people who are located within a five minute drive time caters to people who may be coming from as far away as ten, fifteen, or twenty minutes and more.

**Drawing Power.** Every business needs to know about its drawing power—in this case, the geographic extent of its trade area. Knowing whether your store or restaurant is attracting customers from beyond the nearby surrounding area—the equivalent of three minutes or approximately one mile for neighborhood types of businesses—is important. The further your reach the larger your customer base and potential sales should be.

**Early Termination/Escape/Kick Out Clause.** If you decide to rent space having your attorney incorporate an early termination provision into your lease agreement is the best way to protect the substantial investment you are making. Simply stated, such a clause allows you to terminate your lease obligations prior to the conclusion of either your base term or option term if there is some compelling reason to do so. An example might be a loss of business due to the closing of one or more shopping center anchors. Another might be a substantial increase in the amount of vacant space in a shopping center.

Other reasons for invoking this type of protective clause might be attributable to the continued postponement of needed capital improvements such as roof replacement and parking lot repairs and resurfacing, or common area maintenance problems such as continuous delays in snow removal and the replacement of burned out parking lot lighting. Such problems can result in diminished customer counts.

Having such a clause in your lease can also provide you with a platform for requesting temporary rent relief—something that most good landlords will consider if you have a history of being current with your rent.

Similarly, you need to make sure that you can invoke such a lease clause if your landlord wishes to relocate you to lease space which may not contain the same types of amenities which your present space has—things like substantially similar visibility, store frontage, signing, windows, convenient as well as sufficient parking, building improvements, and interior finishes. In such instances be careful to also not overlook the potential for loss of business due to the lack of synergy or compatibility with one or more adjoining or nearby tenants.

**Ego.** Never, ever let ego get in the way of making an informed site selection decision. That being said, it happens all the time.

**Emotion.** Perhaps the biggest mistake people make in site selection is falling in love with their choice of a particular place or location. There is no room whatsoever in site selection for emotion. Literally, emotion can be likened to a "red flag," the "forbidden fruit," and the "kiss of death." Trust me—"smart" location decisions are made without emotion.

**Employee Parking.** This is less of a problem in suburbia than it is in downtown and neighborhood and older business district settings. In the former instance, parking is usually plentiful and free. However, away from suburbia just the opposite is true.

In instances where customer parking is at a premium employees are encouraged to park off-site. Sometimes on-street parking is available. In other instances, employee parking is available in either no cost or low cost public parking lots. In most instances, however, shared parking with a nearby bank, office, or church can help solve the problem of where employees can park.

In certain instances, locating your business on or near a bus line or mass transit route is another way of addressing the dilemma of employee parking. While not a primary consideration, such access can be especially important in not only attracting but in retaining good employees.

**Employment Occupations.** It is helpful but by no means essential to know what types of jobs your customers have. While some may not be employed at all, good examples are a stay at home mom or dad and retirees, others will be employed in both white and blue collar jobs. Knowing whether your customers are employed in a professional, sales, technical, or clerical capacity can influence the design of your store or restaurant, the types of merchandise or food which is sold, price points, marketing, etc, etc.

**Entrepreneur.** You may think of yourself as being an entrepreneur—something which has its good points as well its bad points. For the most part entrepreneurs are ambitious, hard working people with a huge drive to succeed. They have "can do" attitudes, enjoy challenges, like being their own boss, and frequently question conventional thinking. However, they are also notoriously stubborn.

Two of the biggest drawbacks facing entrepreneurs are their unwillingness to embrace the concept of "team" and their inability to master the art of delegating responsibility. As a result, they sometimes end up being their own worst enemies.

**Exceptions and Excuses.** If you are one of those people who think you can find a "home run" location on your own, then all I can say is please be sure to not only read this guidebook but master the entirety of its contents. Otherwise, I would urge you to seek some kind of professional guidance. Doing so has the advantage of demonstrating that "two heads are better than one." If you don't read and don't absorb the significant amount of information detailed in this guidebook and subsequently decide to go it alone then you must accept full responsibility for your site selection decision. As my old Spanish teacher used to remind us about not having completed our homework assignments, "no hay excusos"—there are no excuses.

**Float.** This is a term which is used to measure unmet opportunity within a neighborhood or community. It is defined as the difference between buying power (demand) and retail or restaurant sales (supply).

**Floor-to-Ceiling Glass.** Most suburban retail stores and restaurants are located in shopping centers where floor-to-ceiling glass is the norm. While this type of glass has advantages for retailers, it is somewhat less desirable for restaurants. In the case of restaurants, it is better to have glass which starts two to three feet off the floor. Doing so affords not only a greater degree of dining privacy, but creates fewer cleaning problems. In addition, having elevated windows can help a business minimize safety problems.

**Focus Groups.** These are an important means of learning about customers as well as for obtaining their feedback. Many companies use focus groups in order to gauge potential customer satisfaction with new products. In other instances, focus groups can be an effective way to learn about customer tastes with respect to such things as desired ambiance, price points, and store and restaurant layouts. The key to relying on focus group input is having a trained and knowledgeable facilitator.

**Freebies (like free rent).** Do not, under any circumstances, take the posture that the site selection decision which you are about to make is dependent on whoever gives you the best deal—for instance two to three months of free rent. Simply put, this is a sure fire method for winning the negotiation battle while losing the sales war. Given the sizable investment in time and money that you will be making the only responsible action is to focus on locations which will produce the most sales revenues not the most savings. On the other hand, if you have done your homework carefully and the site you have chosen is at the top of your list then, by all means, go for it.

**Goodwill.** In many businesses the personality of the owner is responsible for building the types of customer relationships which result in more frequent and higher sales. This is one of those site selection factors which is difficult, if not impossible, to accurately quantify. However, it is essential that you not only recognize its importance, but that you evaluate its impact carefully if you decide to either start, buy, or invest in an existing retail or restaurant business.

**Grand Opening.** The importance of having a grand opening event is lost on many businesses. Why this is the case is somewhat puzzling, especially since it can help to generate not only a lot of positive publicity for your business, but can create name recognition as well as introduce you and what you are selling to lots of potential customers.

At such events, many businesses choose to donate either all or a portion of their sales or profits to a charitable organization. In addition, they present an outstanding opportunity to donate food or prizes and items to local schools, athletic teams, and organizations—some or all of whom might represent a target audience. Almost everybody enjoys going to such gala events, in part because of the socializing and networking opportunities which they present.

**Gravity Model.** This sales forecasting system has been around for a very long period of time. It looks at the size and composition of nearby critical mass in order to determine the trade area of a store or restaurant as well as how critical mass influences customer traffic. Hypothetically, the larger an area's critical mass the further its trade area extends.

**Ground Lease.** In instances where the cost of purchasing real estate is high, or where an owner is unwilling to sell, a ground lease can be an attractive opportunity for retail and restaurant companies to either enter the local market or expand their existing presence. Typically the annual cost of leasing a developed lot is the equivalent of ten percent of its potential purchase price. The catch, however, is that the base term for a ground lease is typically fifteen or more years. This helps to explain why ground leases are not for the faint of heart.

**Guidelines.** Guidelines provide business decision makers with a recommended course of action. Instead of imposing specific requirements, as standards do, guidelines are intended to be instructive. Their purpose is twofold: to minimize mistakes and to maximize opportunities. Every retail and restaurant company needs to build a system for success—something which needs to feature a series of guidelines. The sooner guidelines are identified and put to use the better.

A good example of a site selection guideline is **to open new retail store locations in areas with high concentrations of college graduates.** Another example of a site selection guideline is **to focus restaurant location decisions on securing end caps which provide the opportunity for outdoor dining.**

**High Glass.** See Knee Walls.

**Holdover Clause.** This is an important lease clause that your attorney can help you with. It enables you to temporarily remain in your space for a short period of time (anywhere from a week to two or more months) once your lease has expired. However, in order to invoke this important privilege you will be obligated to pay your landlord a rent premium. Accordingly, count on your holdover rent to increase by as little as ten percent or as much as twenty-five percent or more.

**Judgment.** The odds of securing "home run" locations improve with experience—a lesson which, unfortunately, is lost on too many small businesspeople. "Two heads are better than one" is an old adage which also contains a lot of truth with respect to making "smart" location and "smart" site selection decisions.

In the long run, whether a site selection decision is made by an individual or a real estate committee, the need to do a significant amount of "homework" is absolutely the best foundation for exercising good judgment and for achieving future success.

**Kick Off Event(s).** Every retail company and every restaurant should incorporate a kick off event into their opening for business. When planning for such an event you should think about inviting more than friends and family to visit your new store or restaurant.

Chamber of Commerce officials love attending a ribbon-cutting ceremony. Radio personalities enjoy making remote broadcasts. The local press is always interested in informing their readers about new business openings. And, of course, mayors and city officials cherish the opportunity to welcome new businesses and be the center of attention.

**Knee Walls.** Most shopping centers which are built today feature front facades with floor-to-ceiling glass. This is in sharp contrast to the facades of retail and restaurant buildings which are located in older neighborhoods and urban areas. They oftentimes feature glass which starts at a height of a person's knee. Knee walls add more character to a building—something which has not been lost on the developers of the lifestyle centers which are currently in vogue and are being built all across America.

**Landscaping.** A simple way for retail and restaurant businesses to add curb appeal is to provide attractive landscaping. The provision of a variety of colors which are attributable to the planting of flowers, shrubs, and/or trees, is important. However, be careful to avoid renting a storefront or buying a lot where trees, especially street trees, will end up blocking visibility. While planners and the commissions they advise are correct in wanting to create attractive corridors they sometimes forget that planted too close together street trees can block a store's visibility and therefore negatively impact not only sales, but business longevity.

**Lease Agreement.** This is a comprehensive document which spells out the terms under which a tenant agrees to rent space from a landlord. It is a complex, very detailed, and somewhat intimidating document—something which should definitely be reviewed by a real estate attorney before being executed.

**Leakage.** This refers to money which is being spent in neighborhoods and areas which are different from where people live. Oftentimes this means that people will travel from an underserved area, one with few retail and restaurant establishments, to areas where a cluster of such businesses exist. From a municipality or local government perspective leakage results in lost sales taxes—something which means that less money is available for public services and/or improvements.

**Letter of Intent (LOI).** Proposals and Letters of Intent are synonymous. They identify the terms under which a landlord (Lessor) and a tenant (Lessee) agree to enter into a business relationship. The location and size of space, term, rents, pass through costs, build-out and/or remodeling obligations, hours of operation, tenant improvements, the amount of security deposit and signing form the core contents of a Letter of Intent.

Letters of Intent can be prepared by either a prospective tenant (less frequent) or a landlord (more common) or their respective representatives. Typically they identify a response deadline of five to seven to ten days. In many instances the original LOI is where the negotiation process begins. Accordingly, it is highly likely that a Letter of Intent will be modified in some manner prior to being executed.

Once an LOI is signed, either the landlord or the tenant will provide the other party with a standardized lease agreement. At this point the landlord is likely to insist on obtaining financial statements. Depending upon whether the prospective tenant is a start-up, a small multiunit company, or a regional or national chain, the landlord may ask for authorization to run a credit check.

Because of their detail and complexity, one or both parties is likely to employ legal counsel as a means of advising them prior to executing what typically ends up becoming a revised lease agreement.

**Marketing.** Businesses which budget monies for marketing are much more likely to remain in business than those who don't. Indeed, such businesses are much more likely to increase customer counts and sales revenues. Nowhere is the need for marketing better understood than at the franchise level. Typically, franchisors require franchisees to spend anywhere from three to five percent of their sales on marketing. Thus, a franchisee with annual revenues of $500,000 will be required to spend $15,000-$25,000 per year on marketing. Choosing to spend three to five percent of annual revenues on marketing your business is a good rule of thumb even if you are not a franchisee.

Many different forms of marketing exist. However, effective marketing starts with your understanding something very important—who your target customers are. Afterwards, your objective is to build awareness, create desire, and to get customers in the front door. Once customers visit your business your immediate goal is to keep them coming back. In order to accomplish this you need to commit yourself to constantly promoting your business.

At a minimum, you need to invest some of your marketing budget for print and website advertising. In addition, becoming involved in sponsoring one or more athletic teams or school events is a good way to keep your name in front of people. Doing so is also an effective means for creating both repeat business and loyal customers. Other proven ways for you to market your business include being featured in news articles, creating introductory offers, offering loyalty cards, holding contests, sponsoring family nights, using coupons, periodically offering discounts, and advertising periodic sales.

In some instances you will find that landlords will require that a tenant not only spend money on a marketing program but evidence to them, on a monthly, quarterly or annual basis, just what kinds of marketing initiatives have been undertaken. From a landlord's perspective, requiring that money be spent on marketing is not only in the tenant's best interest, but a proven method for increasing customer traffic at the property which the landlord owns.

**Market Penetration.** Most small businesses, especially mom-and-pop businesses, aren't too concerned about market penetration. Indeed, their focus is on remaining in business. When business owners expand the number of locations they operate they increase market penetration. Doing so enables them to build more name recognition—something which is absolutely essential in order to not only survive but thrive in today's extremely competitive business environment.

**Market Share.** Simply stated, market share refers to the percentage of sales within a market which a restaurant or a retailer captures or owns. By way of illustration, in the hamburger marketplace McDonald's has by far the highest percentage of market share.

**Median.** Median refers to the mid point of a variable like household income or home prices. It is often confused with but is different from the word average (or mean). When looking at demographic data, median is a better reference point than average is.

**Merchandising.** This important term is often associated with how products are displayed. While display is in fact a component, merchandising consists of much more. It incorporates a comprehensive set of influences which are critical to establishing an image and creating a tenant mix which can prompt sales. Developing a merchandising strategy starts with market research, and includes such things as customer profiles, product introduction, packaging, store design, advertising, marketing, gap analysis, demographics and psychographics, and promotion.

**Mystery Shoppers.** Every retail and restaurant business owner who is interested in building repeat business and building either a good or great customer experience should periodically invest a small amount of money to employ the services of mystery shoppers.

These are people who are charged with a very important responsibility: visiting a retail store or restaurant unannounced on one or more occasions for the purpose of recording their thoughts and impressions. Such feedback will subsequently be packaged into one or more report cards and be presented to a business owner.

After receiving mystery shopper feedback business owners will be better positioned to not only understand customer impressions, but be better prepared to make the types of decisions which are critical to not only improving the customer experience but to building an absolutely essential element of success—repeat business.

**Name Recognition.** Chances are the more name recognition your business has the more successful it will become. Therefore, building name recognition should be an immediate focus area both before and after you open your doors for business.

**New.** Today, the word new is a part of our national fabric, something which has become imbedded in our national psyche. As consumers we have become accustomed to buying new cars, new homes, new clothes, etc. This is an important standard to remember and respect if you are either a businessperson or are considering going into business for yourself. Keeping your retail store or your restaurant current is no longer a choice, it is absolutely essential.

McDonald's is a prime example of company that knows the value of making their restaurants look new or current. In many instances they are reinventing themselves by upgrading what were once standard looking (cookie cutter) restaurants into not only richer looking but more welcoming places—places where you can still bring the kids but can also hold business meetings. For McDonald's, periodically spending money on modernization translates into not only increased business but increased profits. If you want to increase sales McDonald's is the model that you should definitely consider emulating.

Another example of a company that understands the meaning of keeping their interiors looking fresh and current is Starbucks. Many mall stores are also super conscientious about having their interiors look new. Mall owners have long understood that **new is oftentimes equated with success**. As such, many of them require tenants to update their stores at least once every five years.

New is, indeed, the "in" look! It is also "money in the bank."

**Niche.** Looking for niches and voids is one way to go about looking for locations and making site selection decisions. While this sometimes means being the "pioneer" in the market it also means that you could initially have the market to yourself.

A word of caution is necessary. Just because a niche or a void exits doesn't necessarily mean that you should make a business investment. Besides making sure that you have a "home run" location, what you need to do is spend time determining the size of the market, estimating potential sales levels, and deciding whether the price you will be paying to rent or to purchase a property will create a reasonable return on your investment.

**Nighttime Businesses.** If your business is evening oriented then it is to your advantage to be near other nighttime businesses. For instance, if you are in the ice cream business, being near a pizza restaurant, a bookstore, or a movie theatre is a good bet to generate additional business.

**Nighttime Visit.** Anyone who is checking out potential locations needs to make one or more nighttime visits to not only the potential site but the surrounding business area. In the process of visiting they should pay particular attention to two important items: nighttime lighting and signing. These are factors which can either negatively or positively influence customer perceptions.

**Numbers vs. Percentages.** When evaluating demographics never, I repeat never, base your impression of a trade area on percentages rather than numbers. For instance, while most everyone would be impressed to learn that seventy percent of the one thousand people living within a trade area earned $100,000 or more in annual income they should be even more impressed to learn that demographics for a competing site indicated one thousand of the two thousand people living within a competing trade area annually earned $100,000 or more. If you do the math, one thousand trumps seven hundred. On the other hand, some people might be misguided into thinking that seventy percent was the more impressive figure.

**Operations.** There are no shortcuts to becoming a good operator. The first step in this important process is on the job training. It is the equivalent of paying your dues. It is something that doesn't happen overnight. Oftentimes this means that you will be starting at the bottom of the ladder and working your way up. This kind of "hands on" training will provide you with invaluable experience. Indeed, it will turn out to be the best teacher that you will ever have.

Good operations are absolutely essential to achieving business success. While not very often thought of as an influential site selection factor the simple truth is that **good sites coupled with good operations can go a long way towards guaranteeing business success**. However, a good site without good operations is largely doomed to failure. The influence of good operations is so strong that it can, in fact, pave the way for average locations to become better locations.

**Overage Rent.** See Percentage Rent.

**Pass Through Costs:** See Triple Net Rents.

**Patience.** If you have ever heard the phrase "patience is a virtue" I hope you took it to heart. All too often new businesspeople are impatient to get going. They want to do something now as opposed to later. This is a dangerous attitude—one which can not only result in a poor site selection decision, but, end up contributing to a lack of business longevity; in other words, business failure. Doing your homework and being not only patient but selective can go a long way towards determining future business longevity; in this case business success.

**Peak Periods.** Every business experiences certain periods when customer visits are at their maximum. For restaurants selling sub sandwiches this is often over the lunch hour. For retailers selling women's clothing the peak period could be either during the day or evening on a weekend. In order to cope with such peak customer traffic and maximize sales opportunities every business needs to make sure that, in addition to appropriate staffing levels, sufficient as well as conveniently situated customer parking exists.

**Pedestrian Friendly.** Most urban areas have neighborhoods and downtowns where people feel welcome to walk to retail, restaurant, and entertainment locations. These are places where the automobile has lost its power of intimidation. However, with the exception of older suburbs and lifestyle centers, very few pedestrian friendly locations can be found anywhere in suburbia.

All great shopping districts, like the Miracle Mile along Michigan Avenue in Chicago, Madison Avenue in New York City, and Rodeo Drive in Beverly Hills feature busy pedestrian friendly streets.

Whether you are in the retail or restaurant business don't dismiss pedestrian friendly locations. They are capable of generating lots of customer traffic morning, noon, and night.

**Pedestrian Traffic.** Pedestrian friendly older business districts and downtowns have long differentiated themselves from suburban business corridors where strip shopping centers and big box stores and huge surface parking lots are the dominant landscape feature. During the past decade, pedestrian friendly lifestyle centers have become an increasingly popular destination, in part because they have been able to recreate the building, street, and sidewalk vernacular which is characteristic of so many older, inviting business areas.

Designed effectively, these welcoming features can collectively encourage pedestrian traffic and help generate high levels of sales—one of the major reasons why many chain retailers and restaurants have increasingly been willing to leave mall and strip shopping center locations.

**Percentage Rent.** While scorned by most small businesses, percentage rent is looked upon as a value enhancement by owners of malls and shopping centers throughout the United States. Consequently, it is a common lease requirement for retail and restaurant companies who wish to occupy prime real estate.

The "bonus" theory behind paying percentage or overage rent is that landlords should be rewarded financially for establishing a synergistic tenant mix—a feature which, if done correctly, should account for higher sales levels. In such situations, in addition to paying a base rent, tenants pay their landlords a percentage of their sales beyond a certain predetermined figure.

For example, a retailer may be required to pay a landlord anywhere from two to seven percent of annual sales revenues exceeding $1,000,000. In instances where said retailer produces annual sales of $1,250,000 and is bound by a percentage rent requirement of five percent, the landlord will end up receiving an additional $12,500 in annual rents. Capitalized at ten percent, this translates into an increase in real estate value of $125,000. That's the power of percentage rent!

Most tenants who end up paying their landlords percentage rent don't do so grudgingly because they are happy to make what is usually either a very good or an excellent return on their investment.

**Perpendicular Building.** Buildings which sit perpendicular to the road often have only one prime location—the end cap space which is closest to the street. Such space maximizes visibility, signing, and parking for its retail or restaurant user. Unfortunately, all of the other spaces in perpendicular buildings are at a disadvantage because they don't have as good visibility, signing, or parking as their end cap neighbor.

Whenever possible, businesses should seek locations in buildings which sit parallel to the street. Doing so will enable them to not only have a much better opportunity for maximizing visibility, signing, and parking, but will likely lead to higher sales levels. Furthermore, chances are pretty good that they will also experience less neighbor tenant turnover—something which can end up reducing customer traffic to a shopping center as well as result in both diminished business and reduced sales.

**Per Capita Income.** This measure of per person income can be a good indicator when comparing the attractiveness or appeal of two or more business trade areas. However, no informed decision should be made based solely on this important statistical factor.

**Pick Up Window.** Many restaurants who don't serve fast food have found that pick up windows are capable of not only increasing customer convenience but can help to build higher sales. Pizza restaurants increasingly are incorporating this type of amenity into both their site and building plans.

It is important to point out that pick up windows, unlike drive thru windows, are not accompanied by menu boards. Furthermore, they do not generate the long lines of vehicles which oftentimes result in traffic stacking during peak periods. On the other hand, be aware of the fact that pick up windows should always be accompanied by a bypass lane and may result in fewer parking spaces being available.

**Pictures.** See Camera.

**Previously Occupied Space.** Not everyone can afford or wants to occupy new space. As a result, a lot of start-up as well as expanding businesses are good candidates to go into used space. You need to be careful, however, when considering these types of locations. This is one instance where you really need to do your homework! There is a reason why some of these sites continue to underperform and ultimately result in a cycle of business failure. With that in mind, the first thing you should do is reread Chapter One in this guidebook: The Six Keys to Consistently Making "Smart" Site Selection Decisions.

Please keep in mind that while low entry costs and cheap rents and sometimes the presence of furniture, fixtures and equipment (FF&E) can be very tempting reasons to consider occupying recycled or older space, they are not sufficient justifications for making an investment, whether big or small. Yet, many start-up as well as existing businesspeople think that they will be able to change this repetitive problem and that they will, despite the long odds, succeed. My experience is that, for the most part, these are overly optimistic and somewhat misguided people who are only fooling themselves. Indeed, given a five year time horizon, many of them will either no longer be in business or will have moved to a different location. So, decide whether you are a risk taker or a gambler. And, remember to "look before you leap!"

In those instances where cheap space and/or low entry costs and/or the presence of FF&E represent too big a temptation to pass up, the best thing you can do is sign a short term lease—nothing longer than three years. And, make sure that your lease contains an escape clause which allows you an early exit if, among other reasons, adequate retail or restaurant sales don't materialize.

**Primary Trade Area.** See Trade Area in Chapter Two.

**Proposal.** See Letter of Intent.

**Property Maintenance.** An oftentimes overlooked influence on retail and restaurant sales is the level of service which is delivered by a property manager. A professional who works on site as opposed to someone who works primarily off site is more likely to keep comprehensive service levels high. Furthermore, a property manager who looks at his or her tenants as "partners" and communicates with them regularly is much more likely to build meaningful long term relationships than someone who is simply an investor or someone who doesn't employ the services of a trained professional. Good working relationships can lead to not only less tenant turnover, but, the necessity to spend fewer dollars on tenant space refurbishment as well as new leasing commissions. As a result, landlords end up saving money.

Most tenants judge property managers and their employees by two things: responsiveness and the quality of the work they do. With the exception of occasional plumbing, heating, and air conditioning problems, very little property management is actually performed inside a tenant's space. Most maintenance responsibilities occur outside, primarily within a property's common areas.

In colder climates snow removal is typically the top winter priority for property managers. Not removing snow in parking areas on a timely basis or not doing a good job of keeping pedestrian access points open and free of ice can not only cost tenants business, but is a sure fire way to create adversarial relationships between tenants and landlords.

During warmer months, landscaping and landscape maintenance, followed by blacktop repair, parking lot striping, and parking lot repair require the most attention. Throughout the year, trash removal and maintaining high levels of parking lot lighting will be a property manager's focus areas.

Regardless of what needs to be done, an effective property manager will take good care of his or her tenants because he or she realizes that not only establishing but maintaining long term tenant relationships as well as maximizing tenant business opportunities is the name of the game—especially in today's very competitive commercial marketplace.

**Public Transportation.** Typically, only a few businesses are dependent upon public transportation for generating any significant amount of customer traffic. Nonetheless, many businesses are dependent on such transportation in order to attract and retain employees. Therefore, some businesses may wish to add securing a location which is either on or close to a bus, rail, subway, or rapid transit line to their list of site selection factors.

**Quantitative Analyses.** Gathering factual information is absolutely essential. The more you can put your hands on the better. Yet, beyond obtaining traffic count information and demographic information very little quantifiable data is ever collected by most small businesses. Make it a point to not make this mistake. Do your homework!

**Questionnaires.** See Customer Surveys.

**Radius.** Typically information is evaluated on the basis of the one, two, and three mile radii which surround a particular site. This is informative information and a convenient way of comparing apples and apples.

I would like to offer a word of caution, however. Don't you or don't let anyone else make the mistake of defining your primary customer trade area simply by assigning it a mile marker. While this is frequently done it is an oversimplification that can lead to false assumptions about future sales. For a more reliable means of determining your customer trade area please see Drive Times in Chapter Two.

**Realtor.** See Commercial Realtors in Chapter Three.

**Real Estate Agent.** This is a person who can provide you with information about lease space, property which is for sale, and such things as comparable rents, traffic counts, competition, lease terms, incentives, etc. Real estate agents can also assist you with contracts, proposals, and negotiations. However, only a minority of real estate agents are qualified to provide you with the kinds of comprehensive site selection guidance which is promoted in this guidebook.

**Recessed Entryways.** Many older neighborhood business districts feature these types of storefronts. Unfortunately, with the exception of some mall stores and some lifestyle centers, recessed entryways have been left out of the design of almost every suburban strip center which has been built during the last fifty years. This is unfortunate because such storefronts are not only more interesting but more inviting. Recessed entryways create additional window display areas as well as more opportunities for window shopping.

While a traditional twenty-foot wide storefront in a shopping center may be all glass, a recessed storefront may contain as much as an additional ten feet of glass. What a great way to increase your business exposure without having to pay any additional rent. This is one of the reasons why I like to classify having extra window area as a bonus opportunity.

Ask yourself which building type would you prefer to occupy? Which building type do you think your customers would prefer to patronize?

**Rent. Always think of rent as a function of sales.** Depending upon the type of business you have and the quality of the location you are considering you should count on paying anywhere from seven to twelve percent of your annual gross sales in rent. If your sales are forecast to be robust then you can afford to be at the high end of this range. Whenever your projections reveal more modest sales then you need to be in either the middle or lower end of this range. If your forecast identifies a low level of sales then realistically you will only be able to afford rents which are either at the very low end of this range or below it.

**Return On Investment (ROI).** Calculating a return on investment is an exercise that very few start-up businesspeople devote any time to. Consequently, they don't have a good handle on whether the money they invest and the profits they achieve will result in a generous, modest or skimpy return on the money they have invested.

A good accountant or a SCORE counselor are two good resources you can turn to for help in calculating ROI. While a low cost of investment might be attractive to many small business owners the only way they can earn an attractive return on their investment dollars is to generate above average sales and profits. With that in mind you might want to keep in mind the old saying "it takes money to make money."

**Royalty Fees.** If you operate a franchise then you will be obligated to pay a portion of your weekly, monthly, or quarterly sales to your franchisor. While these fees are typically locked in there is no harm in trying to negotiate a payment schedule which enables you to start off paying lower royalty fees while agreeing to gradually increase them over time to the standard percentage fee. Doing so will enable you to reinvest more of your sales revenues during the start-up and most difficult phase of your business, which is usually the first three years after you open your doors.

**Sale Leasebacks.** This popular vehicle permits the eventual sale of a retail or restaurant property in exchange for a long term lease. Such transactions permit the seller to receive cash and the buyer to lock in a fixed return on investment. Sale leasebacks are a great way to create win-win opportunities for both parties.

**Sales Per Capita.** This is a simple way for measuring sales on a person-by-person basis. For example, if 5,000 people live within the trade area of a business and annual sales reach $1,000,000 then per capita sales of $200 per person will have been realized.

**Sales Per Parking Space.** This is another important means for measuring sales performance. By way of illustration, if a retail store or restaurant has fifty parking spaces and records annual sales of $1,000,000 then each parking space represents $20,000 in customer sales.

**Sales Per Seat.** If you are in the restaurant business this is a great way for learning the value of each customer seat. If your business seats 100 people and you achieve annual sales of $1,000,000 then each seat represents $10,000 in customer sales.

**Sales Per Square Foot.** Simply stated, this is the amount of annual sales divided by the size of the retail or restaurant space you are renting or own. My personal rule of thumb for projecting retail store and restaurant success is to look at what I call the $100, $200, $300, $400 and $500 per square foot sales levels.

If your business does or is forecast to do sales of approximately $100 per square foot chances are it isn't providing you with any meaningful return on investment. You are most likely paying your bills but don't have a lot of "jingle" in your pockets.

Where sales or forecasted sales are in the $200 per square foot range a business is generally turning a small profit. When sales are elevated to the $300 per square foot level businessespeople should not only be making a decent profit but should be turning their attention to finding one or more additional locations.

If your sales are very good, say approximately $400 or more per square foot, you should not only be thinking about expansion but should begin to diligently pursue the opportunity to franchise your restaurant or retail business.

Should your sales either reach or exceed $500 per square foot you have got a "winner" on your hands. Stated differently, you have created the formula for business success. Given your talent you have the potential for building not only a local chain but one which could potentially grow into either a regional or national chain. Congratulations!

**SCORE.** The Service Corps of Retired Executives is a tremendous resource for both start-up and existing small businesses. If you need help with your business plan or your marketing plan or simply need some real estate advice this is a group you should definitely contact. SCORE is made up of people who have either run their own businesses, been in charge of major departments and divisions for big businesses, or have been successful entrepreneurs.

An added bonus of working with SCORE is their affiliation with the Small Business Administration: the SBA. As a result of both one-on-one and group counseling services, SCORE can be a big help to you in not only applying for but obtaining SBA financing through local lenders.

**Seating.** The question is not how much or how little customer seating you have but what kind of sales each seat generates. Is it $5,000, $7,500, or $10,000 or more per seat? If you don't know the answer to this question then you don't have all of the information you need to better assess the performance of your existing restaurant as well as the potential performance of future restaurant opportunities.

Which kind of customer seating should you provide? Which is better: tables or booths? If you only have one choice the answer is booth seating. Quite frankly, people perceive booths as being not only more comfortable but offering more privacy. Adding booth seating is guaranteed to not only improve the initial impressions that customers have of your restaurant, but, increase the amount of repeat business you do.

Whenever you can add outdoor seating please do so—even if it is only a table or two and just a few seats. During warm weather people absolutely love to eat and drink outdoors, especially when they can indulge in a favorite pastime—people watching.

One piece of advice for restaurants owners: take advantage of every opportunity to maximize window seating for your customers.

**Secondary Streets.** These are streets which are located off of the "main drag," the primary street. Unless you are considering opening a destination business within approximately three hundred feet of the "main drag," you are advised to proceed with lots of caution—especially if visibility from the primary street is less than optimal.

**Second Floor Space.** For retail and restaurants this is the type of space you should avoid—even if it is cheap! Unless located in a mall, only destination-type businesses are likely to survive a second floor location.

**Secondary Trade Area.** See Trade Area in Chapter Two.

**Sensory Appeal.** Some café style businesses have demonstrated that they are capable of creating special places. These are inviting places, places where people not only enjoy coming but want to linger. These are places where everyone feels welcome and comfortable. They are places where individuals are not only happy to meet family and friends but to conduct business.

The opportunity to relax, to purchase food and drinks, and the potential for people watching is a great combination—one which has the ability to create something very powerful, something which is very memorable—an experience. It is this ability to create an experience that not only produces loyal customers but leads to significant sales as well as enhanced profits.

When you are looking for a business location you also need to understand that what you do inside your four walls is capable of playing a very important role in whether your business thrives or simply survives. Accordingly, you are encouraged to pay significant attention to creating an appealing interior design, one which is capable of creating an atmosphere which customers want to experience over and over again. The better you do this the greater the opportunity you will have for building long term business success.

**Service.** See Customer Service.

**Service Drives.** These are easy to spot. They parallel major thoroughfares and usually sit back fifty or so feet from the edge of the street right of way. They have become very popular with traffic engineers because they minimize the number of curb cuts which are permitted along heavily traveled streets. Consequently, they are seen as a safer alternative for accommodating large scale commercial developments and the retail, restaurants, gas, and banks which typically follow.

One of the drawbacks to service drives is that traffic frequently stacks in front of a signalized intersection. This results in drivers sometimes having to wait longer than they would like in order to turn off of the service drive and get in line to be able to turn onto the major thoroughfare. Thus, convenience oriented businesses are not especially well suited to locations on service drives.

The other major drawback associated with service drives is that the green space area which sits in front of them becomes a popular candidate for beautification. This can result in regulators becoming overzealous about requiring street trees to be planted. While street trees may look attractive they oftentimes end up blocking building and signing visibility—something which can negatively impact sales.

**Service Retailers.** Dry cleaners, chiropractic businesses, beauty salons, nail salons, insurance offices, financial/brokerage offices, optical stores, real estate offices, and barber shops are all examples of service retailers. While not glamorous or sexy, they are all good examples of businesses which tend to stay put for long periods of time and routinely pay their rent on or before the due date. Thus, they definitely should not be overlooked.

Two of the qualities of most service retailers are that they do not require a significant amount of off-street parking and are very compatible neighbors.

**Shadow Businesses.** Oftentimes businesses will commence their site selection efforts based upon the success of a "model" business they want to be near. For instance, many businesspeople like to follow anchors such as grocery stores, drugstores, and big box stores like Target, Wal-Mart, and Home Depot. In the quick service and convenience business many companies want to focus their efforts in areas where Panera, McDonald's and Starbucks have a presence.

The thinking on the part of people who want to shadow a business is that they can not only tap into the customer traffic which is generated by one or more of these businesses but, that they can reduce their risk of failure. While such shadowing is understandable and has, in fact, worked for many decision makers, what cannot be overlooked are the possible differences that potentially exist in not only the quality of individual sites but the quality of individual operators. Indeed, **the most successful businesses are always characterized by a combination of quality sites and quality operations.**

**Shared Parking.** In exchange for a small monthly fee some property owners will permit one or more nearby businesses to utilize their parking lot during non peak periods in order to accommodate employee and/or customer overflow parking. Churches, office buildings, and banks are prime candidates for authorizing shared parking. If you decide to pursue such an arrangement please be advised that it is in everyone's best interest to sign an agreement which identifies the terms under which shared parking is permitted.

**Site Plan.** This is something which is relatively easy to obtain. Any property owner or real estate agent should be able to provide you with a site plan. It will show not only how the building you are considering leasing or purchasing is situated on the property but where parking is located, how many parking spaces are available, points of ingress and egress, tenant locations, etc., etc.

**Site Selection.** In order to make an informed decision, the process of site selection requires that a variety of homework be completed by either you or by someone you trust—someone who is knowledgeable about commercial real estate. Selecting productive retail and restaurant sites, especially those qualifying as "home run" locations, is not an easy job or something which can be accomplished quickly. Rather, good site selection demands that a significant amount of effort, including hours and hours of fieldwork, be completed.

After reading through the various chapters of this guidebook your site selection skills should be significantly improved. Accordingly, you can look forward to not only realizing a higher return on your investment but to building a strong foundation for future growth.

**Site Selection Coach.** Many operating small businesses and most start-up retail and restaurant owners would learn a lot if they invested what amounts to a relatively nominal amount of money to hire an experienced and knowledgeable site selection coach. This person need not be a commercial realtor but could be. Your best option may be to employ the services of a real estate consultant. For instance, **Location Decision Advisors** (the author's company) provides this kind of service—a service which need not always be provided face-to-face.

**Site Selection Criteria.** Oftentimes small businesspeople and start-up business owners have only a few general standards to assist them in their site selection search. This can turn out to be a big negative—something which means they may be settling for secondary rather than primary sites.

At a minimum, you should have a list of all of the following requirements. Square footage. Front footage. Window frontage. Preferred tenant mix. Parking spaces. Preferred anchors. End cap/in line/freestanding location preference. Minimum daytime population. Minimum nighttime population. Minimum education levels. Minimum income levels. Minimum traffic counts. Maximum building depths. Also, include special requirements like outdoor seating and glass wrap.

**Site Selection Snob.** This is a term which can be used to describe a relatively small group of people. Site selection snobs are people who have a track record of making "smart" location and "smart" site selection decisions. **They know how to consistently pick winners and avoid losers.** With few exceptions, they work in corporate real estate, commercial real estate brokerage, real estate consulting, and for businesses with multiple locations.

Given his significant experience and track record in real estate, the author oftentimes considers himself, for better or for worse, to be a bit of a site selection snob. Nevertheless, his interest in helping people to succeed remains his greatest satisfaction, his primary joy.

**Site vs. Location.** While often used interchangeably, these words really describe two different types of places. Think of macro and micro. In this case location is the macro and site is the micro. Stated differently, location typically describes an area such as a street, a neighborhood, or a community. Site, on the other hand, refers not only to a specific property but to a specific place (space).

The distinction between location and site is important because **while it is relatively easy to decide on a desired location for your business it is much more difficult and much more time consuming to reach a decision on what constitutes the right site.**

Choosing a location is something that many people are capable of doing. Choosing a site, on the other hand, is something that only a relatively small group of people ever end up mastering. It is important to realize that most small businesspeople fall into the former group and that very, very few of them ever end up being a part of the latter group.

**Small Business Administration (SBA).** The SBA is a division of the U.S. Department of Commerce. Its primary function is to work with small and start-up businesses in order to help them secure conventional financing from a variety of sources, from large regional and national banks to small community banks. What the SBA does is act as a loan guarantor, thus making conventional lending more attractive to the lenders involved. The SBA's involvement also means that the borrower is eligible to borrow a higher percentage of loan monies. Of particular importance to the small business community are SBA's 504 and 7A loan programs.

If you are contemplating becoming a franchisee you should know that the SBA maintains a Franchise Registry. The beauty of having a franchise organization listed in the Registry is that applications can be processed more efficiently and quickly by the SBA and the lenders that it works with.

As mentioned previously in this chapter, SCORE is affiliated with the SBA and offers counseling services to the small business community **prior** to their approaching lenders. You may be interested to know that lenders often refer applicants to SCORE for additional counseling prior to completing the loan application process.

**South & West Facing Space.** If you are looking to be on the "sunny" side of the street—which is usually the preferable side of the street unless outdoor seating is a feature of your business—then you want your entry door(s) and windows to face either south or west. If the entirety of your business is conducted indoors the only two things you need to be concerned about are whether the sun will cause any of your window displays to fade or cause any discomfort for customers who are seated in immediately adjoining window areas. Covered walkways and window awnings are the two most common options for mitigating these concerns.

**Space.** For retail and restaurant business owners who plan on going into multi-tenant space it is not enough that you have already picked the "right location" and the "right site." Now you need to determine whether the in line or end cap space which you are considering will end up maximizing future customer sales.

If you have previously read and applied the advice which is contained in this guidebook you shouldn't have any difficulty making a good decision. However, for those individuals who haven't done their homework it is important that you realize that the odds of making a bad decision will be significantly increased if you have a lack of information or only limited information. While a good decision can put money in your pocket a bad decision can not only take money out of your pocket but can seriously jeopardize your ability to stay in business.

**Space Plan.** Drawing up a floor plan for your business is relatively easy. It should show sales areas, the location of the front counter and cash register, restrooms, kitchen, dining areas, storage rooms, office area, changing rooms, etc.

**Space Size.** Be careful not to bite off more than you can chew. In other words, don't commit to more space than you need. If you are a company with multiple locations or a multi-unit franchisee this won't be a problem. However, knowing how much is enough or too much is often a dilemma for start-up businesses.

If you are in the bakery, dry cleaning, or jewelry business, you typically need space which doesn't exceed one thousand square feet. In the case of chiropractic offices, specialty retail stores, ice cream, frozen custard and yogurt, gelato shops, nail salons, florists, insurance offices, sandwich shops, travel agencies, pizza pick up and delivery establishments, small gift shops, and bagel and coffee shops, spaces which range from approximately twelve hundred to eighteen hundred square feet are generally all the space you need.

The space needs for convenience stores, beauty salons, liquor and wine stores, tanning salons, fast casual, and quick-service restaurants seldom exceed four thousand square feet. Table service restaurants and sports bars need to be bigger—typically ranging in size from four thousand to six thousand square feet. It isn't until you get into categories such as carpet, tile, and golf stores, discount clothing stores, dollar stores, and mattress stores that square footage begins to push ten thousand square feet.

The number of businesses with space requirements ranging from ten thousand to twenty five thousand square feet quickly diminishes. Examples in this category include drugstores, office supply stores, discount clothing stores, and book stores. Beyond this size are the grocery stores. They are followed by "junior" and "big box" stores—businesses which are almost exclusively the province of companies with a regional and/or national presence.

**Storefront Entryways.** Storefronts which stand out due to a variety of designs, building materials, and colors are much more likely to attract customer attention. This is one advantage that many older business districts offer. Today's lifestyle shopping centers are a great example of borrowing from the past in order to enrich the appeal of new retail and restaurant spaces.

Architects and developers who specialize in shopping center design understand that they need to create buildings with unique storefront identities—something which can immediately differentiate them from their neighbors. Unfortunately, interesting and appealing storefronts are not often found in the strip shopping centers which not only dominate today's suburban landscapes but contribute to its sameness, dullness, and oftentimes negative image.

**Street Furniture.** Many communities have invested public monies in an effort to create more attractive business districts. For the most part, adding paver or brick lined walkways, decorative street lighting, attractive trash enclosures, colorful landscaping, a bench here and there, and street trees will not only have a positive visual impact but will almost certainly build curb appeal and help to increase customer traffic.

One word of caution about trees is that they are continuously growing and might eventually end up blocking or partially blocking storefront signs as well as obscuring one or more display windows. Therefore, it is important that you understand that there may be some unintended long term consequences with respect to not only the kinds of trees which are planted but where they are located.

**Subdivision Plats, Building Permits and School Enrollment Projections.** The best way to explain the importance of each of these factors is to mention the quick service (fast food) restaurant behemoth McDonald's. No one does more homework than McDonald's. Their real estate department literally leaves "no stone unturned" when it comes to site selection. This is why so many businesses want to find a location in the same area as McDonald's.

When McDonald's begins its site search it looks at many, many factors. One of these is growth. Therefore, knowing how many new residential subdivisions have been approved, how many lots have been platted and recorded, and how many building permits have been issued is important when projecting future sales levels. The same is true with respect to school enrollment. Finding out whether one or more area elementary, middle, and/or high schools are growing is an important site selection consideration.

Everyone can learn from the McDonald's approach to data collection and sales forecasting. Sadly, many businesses as well as very few individuals will ever consider, let alone utilize, such a time tested approach. This lack of interest in or inability to undertake a comprehensive site and area evaluation helps to explain why business failures will continue to occur in every community.

**Subjectivity.** There is little room for subjective thinking in the site selection process. Instead, you are advised to focus your efforts and your energies primarily on collecting and interpreting factual data—information which is measurable and can be easily compared.

For the most part, subjective thinking is only likely to confuse you or to cloud your thinking. Therefore, you should limit it to the advice of other area businesspeople you have talked to and to your first impressions of a potential retail or restaurant site.

**Surplus Space.** Unless your business can grow into unneeded space within a relatively short period of time you should avoid buying or leasing extra or surplus space. In many instances, landlords have space which is deeper than you require but don't understand that it is not only space you don't have an immediate need for but that you don't want to pay for. Therefore, unless you are offered a shorter base term (for instance, one year as opposed to three years) or either a blended or discounted rate you should avoid signing on the dotted line for surplus space.

Oftentimes small retailers such as bakeries, dry cleaners, and jewelers are unable to find space in a highly desirable location which is no larger than eight hundred or nine hundred or one thousand square feet. Because of this unfortunate circumstance they are often left with a choice: should I or shouldn't I? In such instances you need to consider whether such excess space can be justified from a sales and profit perspective. If it can, then go ahead and lock it up. If it can't be justified then you should consider either extending your site search or try negotiating either a lower rent or securing one or more financial incentives.

**TEAM.** Many times businesses are started by people who want to be their own boss. While there is certainly nothing wrong with wanting to be the master of your own destiny there is one potential limitation: the practice of not relying on others for help. This is where you need to rely on what I like to call a TEAM mentality. Briefly, this important acronym stands for Together Everybody Achieves More.

When you are out scouting locations and sites for your business don't overlook potential resources like commercial realtors and/or site selection consultants. Think about adding such resource groups to your team, much like you would your banker, your accountant, and your attorney. In the long run you'll be thankful because these are people who can help prevent mistakes, especially big time real estate mistakes—the kind that can significantly shorten the duration of your business career.

**Tenant Build Out.** Most landlords typically provide tenants with two kinds of rental space. For new space the standard is a "vanilla" box finish. This typically includes the basics: unpainted drywall, concrete floor, one restroom, ceiling, lighting, electrical outlets, HVAC, and a hot water heater. For restaurants, upgrades in kitchen and restroom plumbing, electrical, and HVAC will all be required—how much depends upon the type of restaurant use.

In certain instances, a landlord may agree to deliver unfinished space or "cold, dark shell" space while providing a build out allowance to the tenant who will then assume responsibility for completing the build out. This removes the landlord from the space planning and building permit processes as well as from bidding the job and hiring one or more contractors.

Older or second generation space is usually delivered to tenants in either "as is" condition or with some minor improvements. Such improvements might include low cost items such as freshly painted walls, new flooring, new ceiling tiles, etc. Alternatively, some landlords will be happy to simply provide a new tenant with some form of free rent in exchange for the tenant coming "out of pocket" to refurbish the subject space.

**Tenant Improvement Allowance.** Landlords will consider providing a desirable tenant, one who has good credit and good financials, with some form of build out allowance. Physical build out is the key. Landlords don't want to spend money for things like furniture, fixture, and equipment. Nor will they consider providing money for decorative items.

Upgrading the HVAC, electrical, and plumbing systems are likely candidates for improvement dollars. Adding glass wrap or an outdoor patio represent other possibilities. These are improvements which ultimately add value to a property. Remember that landlords want tenants to have "skin in the game." In other words, they want to see tenants come out of pocket for a long list of improvements items like flooring, lighting, and painting.

**Third Place Environments.** No company understands how to create a third place mentality better than Starbucks and Panera. These are businesses which encourage customers to not only visit, but, to stay as long as they like, whether that means eating, drinking, reading, people watching, conducting business meetings, spending time on line, or any combination of the above.

Third places are special. They are places where you want to linger, where you want to hang out. They are places where you feel comfortable and welcome and don't want to leave right away. These are places which are designed to make you feel at home, places you want to take family and friends. They are places which breed something which is very important—intense customer loyalty. It is this loyalty which leads to lots of repeat business—something every business wants but doesn't always achieve.

**Trees.** Trees have their place in certain settings. For instance, they are quite commonly used to not only dress up older business districts but revitalize "main streets." In addition, trees help establish character and help provide curb appeal, especially in pedestrian friendly business areas.

Nonetheless, if not properly evaluated, trees can end up creating visibility problems by blocking storefront signs and windows. This, in turn, can end up costing merchants sales and negatively impact their ability to remain in business. Therefore, you need to make sure that something as welcome as a tree doesn't, in fact, turnout to be "hazardous" to your pocketbook.

**Trip Origin.** Understanding where your customers are coming from is very important, especially if you intend to create one or more trade area maps. While most customer visits begin from home, some originate from work, some from visiting family and/or friends, some from school, some from recreational facilities, some from church, some from entertainment, some from restaurants, some from shopping, etc.

**Triple Net Rents:** Most shopping center owners charge their tenants what is known as a triple net rent. Sometimes referred to as pass through costs, triple net rents require a tenant to pay his or her pro rata share of real estate taxes, insurance and common area maintenance.

**Turning Radius.** Determining what is a proper vehicle turning radius into a shopping center or place of business is typically the responsibility of an engineer. Make them too tight and curbs and landscaping are likely to get run over and damaged by delivery trucks and large vehicles. This not only looks unsightly but costs money to fix.

**Two Hundred to Three Hundred Feet Away.** Unless your business is strictly destination oriented and will be located on either an intersecting or parallel street which is already home to a cluster of other nearby retail and/or restaurant businesses, the maximum distance you should consider locating your business off of "the main drag" is two hundred to three hundred feet. Otherwise, locating "just around the corner" means that you are likely to experience a significant drop off in customer traffic in comparison with the amount of customer traffic which either walks or drives by the multiple businesses which account for "where the real action is."

**Urgency.** While the pros are very thorough in conducting the research which is required to make "smart" location and "smart" site selection decisions, oftentimes small and start-up businesspeople are in a hurry to get the ball rolling. Maybe they've been out for a drive and saw something they liked. Or, perhaps a developer or a commercial realtor has contacted them about an opportunity. They may even be motivated by the fact that a competitor is expanding and they don't want to concede a loss of market share.

Please don't be guilty of reacting or making quick decisions with respect to site selection. In site selection, urgency typically leads to mistakes. While there is nothing wrong with finding a location for son "Joey" or for cousin "Vinny" what is important is that you take your time and **follow the advice which is spelled out in this book.**

**Valet Parking.** Casual and fine dining restaurants that are located in areas with limited amounts of on street parking are the businesses which are most likely to offer this type of service. Nearby parking lots, such as those which serve churches, offices, and banks are typical recipients of such "overflow" parking. If offered, valet parking can end up being a big boost to restaurant sales.

In many communities shared parking arrangements are permitted only if two or more property owners sign an agreement and evidence said agreement to local zoning officials. In other instances, zoning will require the issuance of what is known as a Conditional Use Permit—a written authorization which permits shared parking based upon a set of conditions governing such things as days and hours of operation.

**Vanilla Box Space.** Developers and landlords typically deliver space to tenants complete with walls, ceilings, lighting, HVAC, and one or more restrooms. The tenant is then expected to decorate the walls and provide floor coverings. Extras such as additional HVAC, electrical, and plumbing are, along with improvements such as outdoor patios, awnings, signs, and additional glass typically paid for by the tenant.

**Website.** Please don't overlook this important sales tool. Today websites are the single most important investment every small business can make in order to increase not only name recognition but sales revenues.

**Women.** In case you don't already know, women are the key decision makers when it comes to shopping as well as deciding where to go to eat. They tend to not only be more loyal to a particular business than men but attach greater importance to curb appeal, cleanliness, ambiance, and nighttime lighting. If you can, please do not overlook what is important to women. If you do, you definitely risk taking money out of your pocket.

**Written Impressions & Observations.** Whenever you visit a commercial property or talk with a commercial realtor or property manager be sure to have a pen or pencil and paper handy in order to jot down notes, thoughts, or buzzwords. The human mind is a lot more frail than we think, especially when it comes time to processing numerous observations, conversations, and multiple properties.

**Yellow Pages.** This is an expense which is not only costly but is seldom as helpful as one might think. One of the reasons for this is that Yellow Pages advertising is difficult to track. Thus, being able to accurately measure results can turn out to be very challenging.

**You.** Are you ready to go to work? Do you have a business plan? Do you have a marketing plan? Are your finances in order? Is your credit score good? Are you prepared to make a big investment of time and money to open a business?

These are some of the questions you need to ask yourself before deciding to either lease or purchase property. Being thorough and "looking before you leap" are key attributes of people who know what they are getting into and are prepared to meet the challenges of the future.

In the long run, "business success is about doing not only the right things, but doing things right."

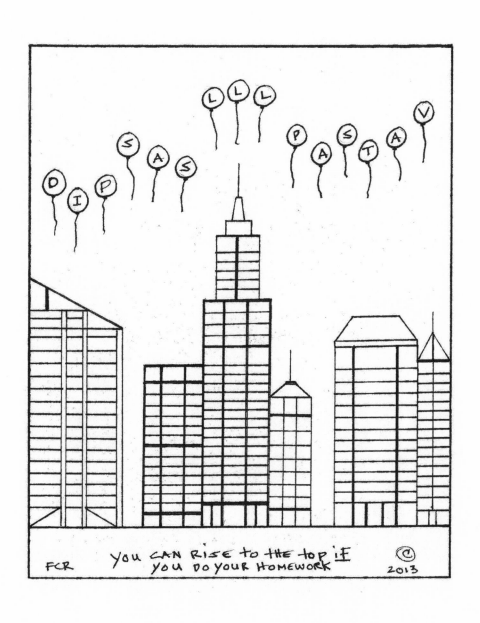

# CHAPTER SIX

## Estimating Retail and Restaurant Sales

Developing a system for accurately estimating future sales is not an easy task. Like site selection, it is part art and part science. It is, however, an extremely important step and something which needs to be completed prior to opening a new business.

Two longstanding and highly reliable methodologies exist for forecasting sales. The first of these is called the **analog** system. It was developed by the Kroger Company many, many years ago and relies exclusively on past sales from stores possessing a series of similar characteristics as well as exit surveys to accurately forecast new store sales volumes.

The other forecasting method is even older. It is known as the **gravity** system. It looks at the size and composition of an area's critical mass to forecast customer sales from the surrounding trade area. Hypothetically, the bigger a geographic area's critical mass the bigger its trade area draw, and, the greater its overall sales. In addition, the gravity model established one of the guiding principles of location analysis: **sales decline with distance.**

Rather than rely exclusively on one or the other of these proven systems the author typically likes to borrow from each of them. In addition, he likes to interject a third consideration—significant amounts of customer information coupled with growth related information—whenever he is involved in projecting retail or restaurant sales.

A reliable sales forecasting system will take many variables into consideration. Each variable has the potential to either somewhat, largely, or significantly influence projected sales.

Knowing as much as possible about your customers is an essential first step. In particular, **you want to learn everything you can about your best and most loyal customers.** While your best customers may only account for a minority of your overall customer traffic counts they are traditionally responsible for a significant amount of your sales.

Important questions you want to learn the answers to include: who are your customers, where are they coming from, how many minutes did it take them to get to your place of business, what did they end up buying, how much money did they spend, how often do they visit, etc, etc.

Demographic and lifestyle factors, along with information obtained as a result of field visits, are another critical component in developing reliable sales forecasts. Once such variables have been identified the real challenge becomes how much weight should be assigned to each of them.

Consider, for instance, which of the following demographic factors should be the most heavily weighted in determining future retail or restaurant sales. Total population (total *number* of people), the *number* of college educated households, the *number* of households with incomes of $75,000 or more, the *number* of homes valued at $250,000 or more, or the *number* of people employed in professional/business/financial and related jobs. By now it should be clear that you need to focus on *numbers* as opposed to percentages!

What you also need to do is **begin looking at which factors are correlated with sales.** Some will be highly correlated while others will have little or no correlation. **Your job is to learn which factors have the most important influence on sales.** Only after you complete this important exercise can you begin building your site selection model.

One of the first things you should do is determine whether there is a correlation between sales and trade area population. Similarly, you should evaluate whether a correlation between trade area households and sales exists.

Next, you need to determine if any correlation exists between sales and a number of important variables. Examples include the number of people possessing a Bachelor's, a Master's, and/or a Professional School Degree, the number of people twenty-five to fifty-four years of age, and the number of people who are employed in white collar jobs—especially in the professional/business/financial segment.

You will also need to determine if any correlation exists between sales and the number of trade area households in certain income ranges such as $75,000—$99,999 or $100,000-$149,999. Other sales correlations might be related to the value of home owner occupied housing (such as those costing $200,000 or more) and the number of daytime employees in an area.

It is also essential to determine what impact both area and site factors have on retail and/or restaurant sales. With respect to the former, you need to determine if any correlation with sales exists for variables such as the size of the nearby critical mass, the number and size of nearby anchor stores, the number of shadow businesses, the amount of competition, and, the type of land use mix in the nearby area.

In addition to determining the correlation between sales and the number of parking spaces serving your business, some secondary site variables which you might add to your evaluation list include: the amount of lot frontage, the amount of store frontage, the amount of building setback, and the amount of synergy with both nearby and adjacent uses.

For those of you who want to delve into micro analysis you might consider such correlation to sales variables as the presence or lack of connectivity to the surrounding area, the local speed limit, the number of moving lanes of traffic, the presence or absence of a nearby traffic signal, and the hours during which significant business activity occurs.

Whether a business is freestanding, in an end cap, or is classified as in line space, the type of space your business occupies will have an impact on sales. In most instances, sales correlations are highest for freestanding buildings and decline for end cap and in line building locations. For evidence of this all you need to do is visit your corner drugstore. Over the last decade drugstores have made a big time switch from occupying end cap building space to locating into freestanding buildings. While a freestanding location, especially one which is situated at a corner and is served by a traffic signal, is going to be expensive the bottom line is that the substantial increase in sales justifies why drugstores have been sold on relocating.

Both a series of non traditional and easily overlooked factors can also influence sales estimates. Gathering information which details the number of new residential lots which have been approved and/or platted, building permits which have been issued, the number of new postal drops, projected increases in school enrollment, new job growth, and attendance at large seasonal attractions such as amusement parks and major sporting events can help explain why you should count on a boost in sales revenues.

Whereas the owner of multiple retail stores or restaurants can reference sales at existing locations in order to project sales for a new location, the start-up business person has no choice but to make a series of assumptions—something which can be a daunting exercise to say the least. Furthermore, estimating sales for a start-up business can be difficult because a new business owner must take into account a factor which is frequently overlooked—a start-up period during which sales may not get off to a fast start. Given these obstacles, the first time business owner has no choice but to be as thorough and realistic as possible.

When making retail sales forecasts, sales per square foot is the best and most common standard for measuring business success. While sales per square foot are also important in the restaurant industry another important variable—sales per seat—also needs to be considered. Whether applied to retail stores or to restaurants, another credible performance measure is sales per parking space.

If you want to consider more sales barometers, some of which are more meritorious than others, you should look to your trade area with respect to sales per resident, sales per household, sales per family, sales based upon the number of people with BA, MA, PhD, and professional school degrees (primarily doctors, dentists, and attorneys), sales based upon certain age groups, sales based on certain income levels, sales based on certain home values, and sales based on the number of persons employed in white collar jobs. The take away here is that **the more ways you have to evaluate sales performance the better.**

# CHAPTER SEVEN

## Creating A Site Selection Scorecard

The purpose of a Site Selection Scorecard is to have a **system** in place for not only looking at, but evaluating various sites. Sadly, besides major retail and restaurant companies, very few people employ such **a systematic means** for making decisions. The reason for this is quite simple: they fail to comprehend the complexity of the decision which they are about to make.

The best advice I can give to someone who is contemplating starting a business or either expanding or relocating an existing business is to employ the services of a professional; someone who is energetic, someone who pays attention to detail, someone you can trust, and most important of all, someone who has not only years of site selection experience but someone who can point to one site selection success after another.

Site selection for the uninitiated is akin to rolling the dice at a gambling table; sometimes you are going to win and sometimes you are going to lose. However, if you use the author's system, or something which is highly similar, you will substantially increase the opportunity to employ a proven, time tested means for evaluating sites. As a result, you will leave behind emotion and urgency—two items which prevent a lot of people from making "smart" location as well as "smart" site selection decisions. And, you will be in a position to more accurately pick winners and avoid losers.

The Site Selection Scorecard which is provided is an *illustration only*. It can be tweaked, especially with regards to the demographic criteria which appear in

Step One. It employs a simple, easy to understand and easy to use point based scoring system. The most positive impression values are worth the most points. Relatively positive impression values are worth the next highest number of points. The least impressive values are worth the least number of points.

This particular Site Selection Scorecard is best used in a suburban setting rather than when evaluating a potential downtown or older business district or dense urban neighborhood. For these types of locations you should depend upon making some slight modifications to the Site Selection Scorecard.

The very first thing you want to do is have an idea of which area within a business district, neighborhood, or community you think can support your type of business. This decision should be based upon looking at such factors as demographics, critical mass, anchor stores, vacancy levels, etc. Afterwards, your choice(s) should be confirmed by driving through as well as around the area which you are considering. Once you are positive that you have found the appropriate area you should complete the following relatively simple exercise.

### STEP ONE: Area Specific *POSITIVE* Criteria

|  | **Positive** |
|---|---|
| *Factor* | *Points Added = 4, 3, or 2* |
| The Presence of One or More Nearby Retail **Anchors** | _____ |
| The Amount of Nearby **Critical Mass** | _____ |
| Nearby **Connectivity** to the Surrounding Area | _____ |
| Nearby **Daytime** Traffic Generators | _____ |
| Nearby **Nighttime** Traffic Generators | _____ |
| Desirable Nearby **Traffic Count** Levels | _____ |
| Nearby **Synergy** Opportunities | _____ |
| The Nearby Presence of Desirable **Land Uses** | _____ |
| The Nearby Presence of Desirable **Population** Levels | _____ |
| The Nearby Presence of Desirable **Income** Levels | _____ |
| The Nearby Presence of Desirable **Education** Levels | _____ |
| The Nearby Presence of Desirable Levels of Daytime **Employment** | _____ |
| The Nearby Presence of Desirable **Age Group(s)** | _____ |
| The Nearby Presence of Desirable **Housing** Values | _____ |

Total Number of *Positive* Points out of 56: +_____

At this point, it is important to clarify what is meant by nearby, both from a demographics and a site perspective. There is some latitude here depending upon the type of business you have. With respect to demographics, nearby for a destination business may well be a three mile radius or a seven minute drive time. For convenience oriented businesses nearby can mean as little as a one mile radius and a three minute drive time. For most businesses, nearby means a two mile radius and a five minute drive time. With respect to site, nearby means close. Typically, this means a distance of no more than one-half of a mile from a site. Personally, the author prefers drive times as opposed to radii when collecting and interpreting data for the simple reason that people's everyday actions are based more on drive times than they are on miles.

Next, you need to look at the impact that the following negative AREA influences will have on your Scorecard.

**STEP TWO: Area Specific *NEGATIVE* Criteria**

| *Factor* | **Negative**<br>*Points Subtracted = 2 or 1* |
|---|---|
| Area **Image** | _____ |
| Corridor **Dynamics** | _____ |
| Excessive **Competition** | _____ |
| High **Speed Limit** | _____ |
| Incompatible **Land Uses** | _____ |
| **Median** Presence | _____ |
| **One Way** Street(s) | _____ |
| Physical or Perceived **Barriers** | _____ |
| Street Construction/Improvements/**Repairs** | _____ |
| Traffic **Congestion** | _____ |

Total Number of *Negative* Points out of 20: - _____

Now you need to **subtract** the Negative Influence score from the Area Specific score in order to arrive at a Total Score. **If the Total Score is 43 or higher then the area you have selected can be regarded as a good or outstanding area.** *However, if the revised score doesn't meet this minimum acceptable point total then, plain and simple, you need to begin looking at other areas for your business.*

While finding the right area should not be a tremendous challenge, finding the right site (or space) will definitely prove to be more time consuming and more difficult. This is where the hard work or fun begins, depending upon your perspective. Keep in mind the fact that, despite what you think the odds are, you are going to find very few "right sites" out there. Indeed, in certain instances finding one or more "right sites" may turn out to be a little like finding a needle in a haystack.

## STEP THREE: Primary Site Specific *POSITIVE* Criteria

|  | **Positive** |
|---|---|
| *Factor* | *Points Added = 5, 4, or 3* |
| **Parking** (On Site & Off Site) | _____ |
| **Accessibility** (Ingress/Egress) | _____ |
| **Signing** (Building & Freestanding) | _____ |
| **Traffic** (Average Daily Volume) | _____ |
| **Activity** (Other Traffic Generators) | _____ |
| **Visibility** (From E, W, N & S) | _____ |

Total Number of *Positive* Points out of 30: +_____

## STEP FOUR: Secondary Site Specific *POSITIVE* Criteria

|  | **Positive** |
|---|---|
| *Factor* | *Points Added = 3, 2, or 1* |
| Adequacy of **Store Frontage** | _____ |
| Adequacy of **Window Space** | _____ |
| **Anchor** Presence | _____ |
| Building **Setback** | _____ |
| **Lighting** Levels | _____ |
| **Pedestrian** Friendly | _____ |
| Tenant **Synergy** | _____ |
| Curb **Appeal** | _____ |

Total Number of *Positive* Points out of 24: +_____

Next you need to look at the impact that the following negative SITE influences have on your Scorecard.

## STEP FIVE: Site Specific *NEGATIVE* Criteria

|  | **Negative** |
|---|---|
| *Factor* | *Points Subtracted = 2 or 1* |
| **Dated** Appearance | _____ |
| Excessive Occupancy **Costs** | _____ |

Excessive **Building Depth** _____
Irregular **Shape** of Space _____
One or More **Undesirable Neighbor Uses** _____
Property **Maintenance** Problems _____
Property **Vacancy** Level _____

Total Number of *Negative* **Points** out of 14: - _____

Now you need to **subtract** the Negative Influence score from the Site Specific score in order to arrive at a final score. **If the Total Score is 42 or higher then the site you have selected is either a good or outstanding one.** *However, if the revised score doesn't meet this minimum acceptable point total then you are advised to begin looking for another site within the same area.*

When it comes time to totaling up your individual Area and Site scores here is what you are looking for:

**"Grand Slam Locations"** = **100 or more points** = **Highest $ Potential**
**"Home Run" Locations"** = **90 or more points** = **Very Good $ Potential**
**"Triple Locations"** = **80 or more points** = **Good $ Potential**

Remember, these are the only three types of locations that you should be paying attention to!

As you can tell from the Site Selection Scorecard process the author recommends finding the right location (area) first and then finding the right site. In addition to objectively evaluating both area and site attributes the Site Selection Scorecard also requires you to objectively assess negative influences—the kind that could easily have a negative impact on future retail or restaurant sales.

This *Five Step Approach* is often overlooked by start-up and small businesspeople. Too many of them mistakenly think that finding a desirable or highly desirable area (location) is all that matters. Somehow they are convinced that it is no longer essential to find and secure the absolute best site within the desired area. WRONG! The truth is that you need to not only find a good area but **you need to secure either an outstanding or a good site if you are going to be in a position to not only compete but succeed.**

The following Site Selection Scorecard evaluation shows how three competing sites in different areas compare with one another. After going through this comprehensive evaluation process you should be in a good position to determine which one or two sites to prioritize and subsequently pursue.

**STEP ONE:** Area *Positives*

| Factor | The Pointe | Buttermilk | Crestview |
|---|---|---|---|
| Anchors | 4 | 2 | 3 |
| Critical Mass | 4 | 2 | 4 |
| Connectivity | 3 | 3 | 4 |
| Daytime | 3 | 4 | 4 |
| Nighttime | 4 | 4 | 4 |
| Traffic Counts | 3 | 4 | 4 |
| Synergy | 4 | 4 | 4 |
| Land Uses | 4 | 4 | 4 |
| Population | 3 | 3 | 4 |
| Income | 4 | 3 | 3 |
| Education | 4 | 3 | 3 |
| Employment | 3 | 4 | 4 |
| Age Groups | 4 | 3 | 3 |
| Housing | 4 | 3 | 3 |
| TOTAL POSITIVE POINTS: | +51 | +46 | +51 |

**STEP TWO:** Area *Negatives*

| Factor | The Pointe | Buttermilk | Crestview |
|---|---|---|---|
| Image | 0 | -1 | 0 |
| Dynamics | 0 | -1 | 0 |
| Competition | 0 | 0 | 0 |
| Speed Limit | 0 | 0 | 0 |
| Land Uses | 0 | 0 | 0 |
| Median | 0 | 0 | 0 |
| One Way | 0 | 0 | 0 |
| Barriers | 0 | 0 | 0 |
| Repairs | 0 | 0 | 0 |
| Congestion | 0 | -1 | 0 |
| TOTAL NEGATIVE POINTS | 0 | -3 | 0 |

| STEP #1 *Minus* STEP #2 = | +51 | +43 | +51 |
|---|---|---|---|
| **AREA CONCLUSION:** | **Outstanding** | **Good** | **Outstanding** |

**STEP THREE:** *Primary Site Positives*

| Factor | The Pointe | Buttermilk | Crestview |
|---|---|---|---|
| Parking | 5 | 4 | 5 |
| Accessibility | 5 | 4 | 5 |
| Signing | 5 | 4 | 5 |
| Traffic | 4 | 5 | 5 |
| Activity | 5 | 5 | 5 |
| Visibility | 4 | 4 | 5 |
| TOTAL POSITIVE POINTS | +28 | +26 | +30 |

**STEP FOUR:** *Secondary Site Positives*

| Factor | The Pointe | Buttermilk | Crestview |
|---|---|---|---|
| Frontage | 3 | 3 | 3 |
| Windows | 2 | 2 | 3 |
| Anchor | 3 | 3 | 3 |
| Setback | 3 | 2 | 3 |
| Lighting | 3 | 3 | 3 |
| Synergy | 3 | 2 | 3 |
| Pedestrian | 3 | 2 | 3 |
| Appeal | 3 | 2 | 3 |
| TOTAL POSITIVE POINTS | +23 | +19 | +24 |
| STEP #3 *Plus* STEP #4    = | +51 | +45 | +54 |

**STEP FIVE:** *Site Negatives*

| Factor | The Pointe | Buttermilk | Crestview |
|---|---|---|---|
| Appearance | 0 | -1 | 0 |
| Costs | 0 | 0 | -1 |
| Building Depth | -1 | 0 | 0 |
| Space Shape | -1 | -1 | 0 |
| Neighbor Uses | 0 | 0 | 0 |
| Maintenance | 0 | -1 | 0 |
| Vacancy | -1 | 0 | 0 |
| | | | |
| TOTAL NEGATIVE POINTS | -3 | -3 | -1 |
| STEPS #3 & #4 *Minus* Step #5 | +48 | +42 | +53 |
| **SITE CONCLUSION:** | **Outstanding** | **Good** | **Outstanding** |

| AREA + SITE SCORE | +99 | +85 | +104 |
|---|---|---|---|
| CONCLUSION: | "Home Run" Location | "Triple" Location | "Grand Slam" Location |

The evaluation system which has been described permits a certain level of subjectivity. However, what is important is that you don't allow emotion to replace objectivity. You need to complete your evaluations with a level head. Sometimes getting a second opinion is the best thing you can do to remain objective.

When making evaluations you might consider looking at aerial photographs in order to get a heightened overview of the site as well as the surrounding area. In addition, you should be talking with area businesspeople in order to gain a better understanding of both the site and the area that you are contemplating making an investment in.

Commercial Realtors who are not directly involved in listing the subject property represent another potential information resource. And, if you feel compelled to discuss your interest with more resource people, you might consider talking with a knowledgeable lender, a local developer, a commercial appraiser, and one or more local property owners.

By employing the scoring system which has been identified a person will be able to more easily determine what constitutes a "home run" location as well what can be classified as a "triple" location. In rare instances, you may even come across what the author likes to call a "grand slam" location. These are very special types of opportunities. They consist of not only an outstanding site but an outstanding area. For classification purposes these are the A+ type of locations—the kind which not only represent a very strong and enviable foundation for future growth, but which have the capability of preventing your competition from locking up superior sites.

"Triple" locations consist of good sites in what can be classified as either good or outstanding areas. They should, along with "home run" and "grand slam" locations be the only types of locations that you move forward with. In order to avoid almost certain failure you should look past what constitutes the great majority of retail and restaurant locations that periodically become available—the so called "double" and "single" locations. Even if the rent is cheap, the opportunity for immediate occupancy exists, and/or the site is close to where you live, please do not consider keeping any subpar locations under consideration. If you do, you will be guilty of ignoring the substantial amount of advice which this guidebook provides.

In conclusion, if you feel that the Site Selection Scorecard information which has been described is somewhat overwhelming please don't panic. It is, indeed, a lot of information to absorb—something that very few people will fully comprehend the first time they read through it. As a result, don't shy away from rereading this important information over again, or, perhaps even over and over again!

---

While this chapter showcases a *Suburban Site Selection Scorecard*, similar scorecards can and should be developed for evaluating *Older Business District, Dense Neighborhood and Downtown locations*. While the scorecard format will remain the same, some new variables should be added while some previously identified variables need to be deleted.

Perhaps the most challenging scorecard to create is one which I haven't mentioned yet; the *Mixed Use Site Selection Scorecard*. Given the increasing popularity and pronounced growth of mixed use development, creating such a scorecard should become a priority.

Depending upon location, today's mixed use developments can range in size from just a few acres in urban settings to 100 acres or more in greenfield areas. They can vary widely, not only in cost but in the variety of land uses which are represented. And, depending upon location, their form can be vertical, horizontal, or a mix of both.

A distinguishing feature of many urban mixed use developments is that, in addition to the ubiquitous automobile, they are likely to be served by alternative forms of mass transportation such as subways, light rail, and streetcars. Two of their other distinguishing features are the creation of pedestrian friendly environments and public open space—places where people can gather for a wide variety of purposes. Here, amenities such as water, outdoor seating, park like settings, wi-fi, and programmed activities which promote venues ranging from concerts to farmers markets, are counted on to attract people as well as add a little "sizzle."

Good design is one feature of mixed use developments which absolutely cannot be compromised. No matter their size, scale, or character, the design of buildings and their core uses is paramount to creating not only a "wow" factor, but acceptance in the only real test that matters—the very competitive marketplace.

In the future, well thought out and well designed mixed use developments will play an important role in suburban growth and in the renaissance of our cities. Done correctly, mixed use will be a catalyst for further capital investment and tax base enhancement. Done unimaginatively, mixed use will act as a deterrent to new development.

# CHAPTER EIGHT

## The Importance of Demographics and Psychographics

While the author believes that too many people initially pay too much attention to demographics he sees demographics as an essential element in being able to make either a "smart" site selection or "smart" location decision. However, regardless of how good demographics look they do not replace the need to do both area and site evaluations. Doing these is the only way that you will ever be able to find one or more "home run" locations.

Demographics can be ordered from many different market research companies including Claritas, Pitney Bowes, Sites USA, and Buxton. Another good source for this important information are the commercial realtors who are actively involved in listing, leasing, and selling properties in one or more of the business areas that you either are or will be evaluating. Keep in mind that if you are only interested in looking at zip code related information you should be able to find what you need at your local library.

Demographics are based upon United States Census information and are updated periodically by companies such as Claritas in order to offer customers current information as well as much in demand demographic projections. They consist typically of multi-page reports which go into significant detail about the study area population and a wide variety of its characteristics. In addition, demographic packages will include a variety of informative maps.

In order to compare "apples and apples" most people like to rely on radius maps and radius reports in order to gain a comprehensive insight into a particular area. Obtaining one, two, and three mile ring information can provide an individual or a company with a wealth of information. Similarly, drive time information can prove equally informative and be very rewarding.

While real estate, market research, and businesspeople who rely on demographic reports will comprehend their contents, many start-up and small businesspeople are intimidated by the scope of the information they contain. For the uninitiated, demographic reports can be somewhat overwhelming. This is one of the reasons why you should consider working with a professional—either a consultant or a commercial realtor—when you are about to become involved in the site selection process.

When you look at demographic reports you want to **pay particular attention to numbers as opposed to percentages.** While percentages can wow you the bottom line is that they don't do a very good job of educating you. So, be careful.

The beauty of demographic reports is that they identify lots of variables. Your job is to determine which of them is the most relevant to your site selection criteria or model and then use them to compare one or more existing locations with one or more potential locations.

What follows is a comparative analysis for three different shopping center sites. The information which is provided is for a **two mile radius** around each site and identifies what the author considers to be the most relevant set of variables. The source of this detailed information is Claritas.

| Demographic Variables | Long Cove | Buttermilk | The Pointe |
|---|---|---|---|
| 2013 Projected Population | 29,996 | 17,016 | 20,969 |
| 2008 Population Estimate | 26,564 | 17,276 | 20,476 |
| 2000 Population | 21,271 | 18,026 | 20,009 |
| 2008 Est. 0-9 Age Population | 4,058 | 2,230 | 3,116 |
| 2008 Est. 10-17 Age Population | 3,456 | 1,817 | 2,719 |
| 2008 Est. 18-24 Age Population | 2,034 | 1,405 | 1,779 |
| 2008 Est. 25-34 Age Population | 3,518 | 2,212 | 2,417 |
| 2008 Est. 35-44 Age Population | 4,803 | 2,225 | 3,193 |
| 2008 Est. 45-54 Age Population | 4,117 | 2,881 | 3,394 |
| 2008 Est. 55-64 Age Population | 2,325 | 2,325 | 2,243 |

| | | | |
|---|---|---|---|
| 2008 Est. 65+ Age Population | 2,155 | 2,181 | 1,616 |
| 2008 Est. Pop. With Bachelor's Degrees | 5,815 | 2,903 | 3,294 |
| 2008 Est. Pop. With Master's/Phd's | 2,417 | 1,259 | 1,337 |
| 2008 Est. Pop. With Profess. Degrees | 506 | 432 | 190 |
| 2008 HH Income $ 50,000-$ 74,999 | 1,928 | 1,512 | 1,496 |
| 2008 HH Income $ 75,000-$ 99,999 | 1,869 | 1,014 | 1,408 |
| 2008 HH Income $100,000-$149,999 | 2,489 | 1,175 | 1,732 |
| 2008 HH Income $150,000-$249,999 | 1,023 | 603 | 529 |
| 2008 HH Income $250,000+ | 301 | 475 | 282 |
| 2008 Pop. Employed in Mgt/Bus/Finan | 3,403 | 2,012 | 2,220 |
| 2008 Pop. Employed in Prof & Related | 3,948 | 2,286 | 2,810 |
| 2008 Pop. Blue Collar Employment | 1,833 | 1,304 | 1,834 |
| 2008 Pop. White Collar Employment | 11,543 | 7,166 | 8,467 |
| 2008 Own. Occ. Hous. $100-149,999 | 1,654 | 1,280 | 1,414 |
| 2008 Own. Occ. Hous. $150-199,999 | 2,027 | 1,075 | 1,883 |
| 2008 Own. Occ. Hous. $200-299,999 | 2,302 | 1,027 | 1,675 |
| 2008 Own. Occ. Hous. $300,000+ | 1,439 | 836 | 577 |

One thing the author learned a long, long time ago was to *pay special attention to the number of people living in close proximity to the site.* Typically the more people the better. In the above example, Long Cove not only has the largest surrounding population but arguably the most appealing demographics to the high end ice cream shop that the author was assisting with site selection.

Another means of analyzing potential locations is to obtain drive time demographic information. The information which follows is from Claritas and is based on a **seven minute drive time** from the two sites that a cafe that I was working with was considering.

| *Demographic Variables* | *Oakley* | *Wyoming* |
|---|---|---|
| 2014 Projected Population | 76,697 | 41,480 |
| 2009 Population Estimate | 77,219 | 42,320 |
| 2000 Population | 78,165 | 44,141 |
| 2009 Estimated 0-9 Age Population | 9,187 | 5,378 |
| 2009 Estimated 10-17 Age Population | 7,207 | 4,651 |
| 2009 Estimated 18-24 Age Population | 7,101 | 3,531 |
| 2009 Estimated 25-34 Age Population | 11,497 | 4,466 |
| 2009 Estimated 35-44 Age Population | 12,257 | 5,552 |
| 2009 Estimated 45-54 Age Population | 11,155 | 6,895 |

| | | |
|---|---|---|
| 2009 Estimated 55-64 Age population | 8,620 | 5,293 |
| 2009 Estimated 65+ Age Population | 10,196 | 6,553 |
| 2009 Est. Population with Bachelor's Degrees | 12,685 | 4,942 |
| 2009 Est. Population with Master's/PhD's | 5,544 | 2,729 |
| 2009 Est. Population with Profess. Degrees | 1,992 | 817 |
| 2009 HH Income $ 50,000-$ 74,999 | 6,317 | 3,119 |
| 2009 HH Income $ 75,000-$ 99,999 | 3,541 | 1,733 |
| 2009 HH Income $100,000-$149,999 | 3,673 | 1,918 |
| 2009 HH Income $150,000-$249,999 | 1,915 | 1,069 |
| 2009 HH Income $250,000+ | 1,204 | 493 |
| 2009 Pop. Employed in Mgt/Bus/Finan | 6,858 | 3,105 |
| 2009 Pop. Employed in Prof & Related | 10,428 | 4,702 |
| 2009 Pop. Blue Collar Employment | 6,527 | 4,499 |
| 2009 Pop. White Collar Employment | 27,895 | 12,833 |
| 2009 Owner Occ. Housing $100,000-$149,999 | 4,919 | 2,852 |
| 2009 Owner Occ. Housing $150,000-$199,999 | 3,009 | 1,263 |
| 2009 Owner Occ. Housing $200,000-$299,999 | 2,543 | 1,136 |
| 2009 Owner Occ. Housing $300,000+ | 3,314 | 1,431 |

In comparing the two sites it is apparent that within the seven minute drive time area the Oakley location is substantially denser than the Wyoming location. However, from a café perspective what further reinforces the attractiveness of this location is the substantial difference in the **number** of college educated people, affluent households, people employed in white collar jobs, and people living in expensive homes.

Before jumping to the conclusion that demographics don't lie and that the Wyoming location doesn't begin to compare with the Oakley location you need to remember that demographics constitute only a portion of the information which you need to evaluate. Sadly, over many years of being involved in site selection I have seen too many people use demographics as the primary reason for choosing a particular location. These are people who didn't understand that you can't afford to take shortcuts when making a site selection decision. They are people who naively believed in **the KISS principle—Keep It Simple Stupid. In site selection there is absolutely no room for this oft quoted principle.**

Getting back to the seven minute drive time demographics comparison for Oakley and Wyoming, you are advised to get out your Site Selection Scorecard and use it as the basis for making your decision. In the meantime, make sure that you go back to Chapter One and reread the Six Keys To Making "Smart"

Site Selection Decisions." Adhering to the PASTA V approach will help to keep you out of trouble.

In the meantime, deciding whether radius or drive time based demographic information is used to help guide the site selection process is a decision which you will need to make. However, regardless of which type of demographic information gets used you can take satisfaction in knowing that the variables you end up evaluating will remain the same.

---

Psychographics offer an invaluable insight into consumer spending habits. They define lifestyles—how people choose to spend their money. Psychographics provide both new and expanding businesses with the opportunity to not only understand who their customers are, but where they shop, where they eat, what they read, what they buy, and the list goes on and on.

Psychographics are a powerful and influential decision-making tool. Unfortunately, not a lot of commercial realtors and small businesses rely on psychographics when making important decisions. This is not because of high costs or lack of availability. Rather it is due primarily to the fact that unlike demographics, psychographics have not yet become a household word.

Because psychographics provide tremendous consumer insights the author has previously relied upon PRIZM information when completing consulting assignments and believes that they should be a part of every site selection evaluation.

PRIZM is a proprietary system which has been developed by Claritas. Using Census information, PRIZM provides users with a variety of segmentation information which describes and groups customers according to lifestyle behavior. All together nearly seventy lifestyle segments have been identified and ranked according to a series of socioeconomic factors which have been given interesting, colorful, and memorable names.

The very top PRIZM customer group is **Upper Crust**. It is the wealthiest lifestyle group in America. It is home to empty nester couples age 55 and older. No group has a higher concentration of residents earning over $200,000 annually or possessing a postgraduate college degree. Only about 1.5% of all U.S. households are classified as **Upper Crust**.

**Blue Blood Estates, Movers and Shakers, Young Digerati**, and **Country Squires** round out the Top 5 most affluent PRIZM groups. Collectively they account for only about 5.71% of all U.S. households.

Other desirable PRIZM groups which high end retailers and fancy restaurants would like to be able to claim as part of their customer base are **Winner's Circle, Money and Brains, Executive Suites, Big Fish/Small Pond**, and **Second City Elite**.

According to Claritas, the three largest lifestyle groups—**Traditional Times, Simple Pleasures**, and **Back Country Folks**—account for approximately 7.61% of U.S. households. The first two of these segmentation groups rank in the middle of the pack, meaning that their affluence level skews average. However, the last PRIZM group ranks at the lower end when it comes to incomes.

In order to give you a better insight into the different kinds of lifestyles which exist in the United States the author has chosen to identify a randomly selected listing of PRIZM groups based upon income levels. Each group features household index scores. An index score of 100 indicates the norm or average while increased index scores identify higher than average patronage.

**New Empty Nests:** Lifestyle Group #14—listen to all news radio (230), belong to a country club (222), order from Lillian Vernon catalog (186), watch tennis on television (178), own vacation/weekend home (175).

**Pools & Patios:** Lifestyle Group #15—buy from the Home Shopping Network (280), read **Kiplinger's Personal Finance** magazine (223), listen to Oldies radio (166), enjoy cruise ship vacations (159), watch soccer on television (153).

**Bohemian Mix:** Lifestyle Group #16—shop at Banana Republic (233), buy from Dunkin Donuts (163), shop at Victoria's Secret (163), watch MTV (155), buy rap music (151).

**Kids & Cul de Sacs:** Lifestyle Group #18—shop at Disney Store (272), watch Nickelodeon on television (264), go to the zoo (248), rent videos (207), shop at Kohl's (189).

**Home Sweet Home:** Lifestyle Group #19—read Inc. magazine (202), go downhill skiing (197), eat at the Cheesecake Factory (189), listen to alternative rock radio (186), member of frequent flyer group (164).

**Gray Power:** Lifestyle Group #21—order from Reader's Digest Association (229), enjoy foreign travel by bus (177), play bingo (161), contribute to PBS (145), read *Golf Digest* magazine (136).

**Young Influentials:** Lifestyle Group #22—read Maxim (216), watch VH 1 (176), eat at TGI Friday's (151), order from Barnes & Noble (150), shop at TJ Maxx (132).

**Suburban Sprawl:** Lifestyle Group #30—listen to classic hits radio (191), read *Road & Track* magazine (181), eat at Pizza Hut (142), watch pay per view sports (141), shop at Old Navy (138).

Like demographics, psychographic information can be ordered either by drive times or radii. And, like demographics, psychographics can be used to establish something which is very important—customer profile information. Collectively, demographics and psychographics arm the small business owner with crucial market intelligence. The author regards demographics and psychographics as extremely important tools for building a success story in today's constantly changing and increasingly competitive marketplace.

# CHAPTER NINE

## Short and Long Form Customer Surveys

One of the most disappointing things about small retail and restaurant businesses is how little they actually know about their customers. If there is any group that needs to know as much as possible about exactly who their customers are it is the small business community. Big companies know their customers—that's one of the reasons why they are big companies.

Why has collecting customer information been so often overlooked by so many small business owners? The primary answer is because it is something that very, very few of them have ever had direct experience with or been trained in. The other primary answer is cost. Quite frankly, most small businesses don't think about spending money on research. This rationale is one of the reasons why so many small businesses are destined to never become bigger businesses.

If your restaurant sells pizza and offers delivery you have a lot of very valuable customer information at your fingertips. For instance, you know who your delivery customers are and where they live. You know how much they spend and how often they had pizza delivered. As a result, it should be very simple to collect and analyze such data. In addition, you can now create something which is absolutely essential—customer spotting maps. You don't need to stop here, however. Armed with such information you can create a series of illustrative charts and graphs. By doing these simple things you will be "head and shoulders" above your competition.

I like to regard such information as market intelligence. Collecting data is not rocket science. Rather it is something that every business owner can accomplish relatively easily and relatively inexpensively. The beauty of market intelligence is that it allows you to understand who your customers are and what their buying habits are. I can't tell you how many times over the past twenty-five years I've asked small business owners to tell me who their customers are and have either received a blank stare or have received only a very general response. They just don't know. Sadly, the "light bulb" has never gone off.

I love customer surveys because they allow me to build a preliminary customer profile. And, once I add in demographic and psychographic information, I can finalize my customer profile. Doing so gives me not only a vital insight into my current customer base but the opportunity to begin looking at where I can replicate the same type of customer base. Ladies and gentlemen, this is the foundation upon which "smart" location and "smart" site selection decisions are made!

Having a profile of exactly who my best customers are puts me in a unique competitive position. It allows me to look at specific geographic areas where, if I can locate the right site(s), I can confidently look forward to opening a second or a third successful retail store or restaurant. And, if I'm either a good or a great operator, I should be able to turn the location that I have chosen using my Site Selection Scorecard into an even better performing location.

Once you begin expanding, you need to continue conducting customer surveys. Don't expect that every location is going to generate exactly the same type of customer. However, what you are after is being able to discern common similarities and overlaps in customer characteristics. Doing so will allow you to sharpen your customer profile focus and to do an even better job of site selection in the future.

Possessing market intelligence information also enables you to eliminate guessing. It also means that you will no longer need to be dependent upon blanket marketing and advertising in order to reach existing and potential customers. Now, you can take a "rifle" as opposed to "shotgun" approach to reaching the people who live and work in your trade area. In the meantime, you can take satisfaction in knowing that most of your competitors will likely continue missing the mark with respect to not only marketing and advertising but site selection and profitability.

Short form customer surveys can be designed either in house or by a company which specializes in market research. The same choices exist with respect to administering long form customer surveys as well as analyzing their results. While budget is oftentimes the deciding factor on how you wish to proceed, the most reliable information comes from employing professionals.

I typically favor randomly sampled exit surveys—the kind where a customer is asked several important questions on their way out the door. Most people will feel complimented that you are asking them to help you out, and, will be willing to answer a short list of questions. Nonetheless, you cannot expect their cooperation unless you postpone their exit for no longer than thirty to forty-five seconds.

While men are certainly capable of administering customer surveys, I prefer hiring females to complete this important assignment. People are more willing to talk to a woman than to a man. Also, they are more likely to say yes to a smiling person—someone who is polite, dressed in a professional manner, and typically young as opposed to being middle age or older.

Short form surveys start with two observations that precede any introductions or questions. The first observation notes a person's sex; are they male or female? The second observation has to do with race; is the person Caucasian, Oriental, Native American, or African American?

Next, I like to find out what food item or retail item they purchased and how much they ended up spending? Afterwards, I like to find out where exactly they came from prior to visiting the subject restaurant or store? Was it from home, from work, from shopping, from a restaurant, from visiting a friend, or, from being at some form of entertainment like the cinema, a play, a concert, or perhaps a sporting event?

I always want to know approximately how many minutes (five or fewer, six to ten, eleven to fifteen, more than fifteen) it took someone to get to the subject restaurant or retail store. This is one of the single most important questions that customers will be asked to respond to.

As I near the completion of the exit survey, I like to find out how many times a year the person being interviewed has been a customer? Is it weekly, monthly, quarterly, twice a year, annually, or longer since their last visit? If you are asking yourself why the responses to this question are so important the answer is simple: you need to know who your repeat customers are. They, as opposed to the very occasional customer, are the people you want to target. They are the ones you want to reward. Indeed, they are the ones who will provide you with the best platform for growing and expanding your business.

Now, for the hard questions. You want to find out the age group of the person you are interviewing. Generally, age groups can be broken down in the following manner: under twenty-five, twenty-five to thirty-four, thirty-five to forty-four, forty-five to fifty-four, fifty-five to sixty-four, and sixty-five and older. Next, you want to ask them what street they live on and what is the nearest cross street? (If you wish, you can also ask them for their zip code.) The responses to this essential question will not only help determine the size and the extent of your customer trade area but will enable the preparation of a highly informative customer spotting map.

The last question is one that you won't end up asking. Rather, it is one where you will show them an index card with various income groups identified and ask them which one best describes their current annual household income. The following illustrate the various income groups they could be selecting from. Less than $25,000, $25,000-$49,999, $50,000-$74,999, $75,000-$99,999, $100,000-$149,999 and $150,000 or more.

Why is this information so important? The answer is really quite simple: you are hoping to create a customer profile. This important information will enable you to not only know the answer to the question who is your customer but, you will now have an accurate tool for helping assess the potential of other locations and sites if you decide to open more businesses.

If you are wondering how many interviews constitute a valid sample I would say that largely depends upon your customer count. Generally, I like to base my analysis on no fewer than fifty to seventy five customer surveys. However, I support the overworked phrase "the more the better" when it comes to increasing the number of responses.

At this point, you are probably asking yourself two very important questions: is there a best day of the week to complete my short form customer surveys, and, is there a certain time during the day or evening when customers should be participating in such surveys?

The answer to both of these questions depends upon the type of business you are operating. Most lunch time oriented restaurants such as sandwich shops will want to take advantage of when the great majority of their customers are present. On the other hand, restaurants which do a substantial amount of dinner business will want to conduct their surveys during the evening. Retailers have the luxury of conducting surveys over a longer period of time, such as from late morning to early evening.

For the most part, late week and weekends trump early weekday periods for conducting surveys, primarily because most restaurants and the majority of retail stores see their customer traffic peak late in the week and on weekends as opposed to during the early part of the week.

If you are interested in learning only one or two things about your customers, like how many minutes it took them to get to your business or what their zip code is, you can ask them these questions at the cash register while they are checking out. If you are interested in learning a little more about them then you might consider having them complete a short five to seven or seven to ten question survey after they have sat down and placed their food order. Afterwards offer them a free beverage, salad, or desert as a thank you for their participation.

If you are in the pizza delivery business you already have a wealth of point of sale information that you can mine in order to learn a whole lot about your customers. Neglecting to assemble, review, and analyze such information is inexcusable. On the other hand, I'm willing to bet that outside of defining their delivery area most people who are in the pizza business have never invested either the time or the money to harvest such data.

Other avenues for collecting customer information are telephone interviews, drawings, contests, and customer loyalty cards. While different venues will end up producing different levels of information, they are all valid exercises for learning more about not only who your customers are, but who your **best** customers are.

Regardless of what type of survey instrument you decide to use, you need to assure each respondent that all of the information which has been gathered will be held in the strictest of confidence.

While long form surveys should be distributed to a random sample of customers at your retail store or restaurant they are intended to be completed at home within a stated time frame such as three to five days.

In order to prompt widespread customer interest in completing each of the twenty plus questions that should be contained in the long form survey, it is common practice to reward your customers with some kind of a gift certificate, purchase discount, or cash. These rewards are something which your customers will be eligible to earn only after they personally return the completed long form survey to your place of business.

Today, it is not uncommon for both restaurants and retailers to ask their customers to complete some type of internet survey. This is a very convenient way for customers to provide important feedback. And, it is also a great way for business owners to provide customers with some form of "reward" for their time and thoughts.

Each long form survey is intended to build upon the information which is contained in the short form survey. However, each of the observation items which appear in the short form survey will need to be asked as questions in the long form survey.

Like the short form survey, the information which is contained in the long form survey is meant to remain confidential. Therefore, the name and address of the respondent is not absolutely necessary.

The long form survey should start off by telling the person who is completing it what its purpose is. For instance, "Your survey responses will be combined with those from other customers to help us better identify who our customers are, what our customers like, and the quality of their experience." It may go on to state that "The responses which are provided will help influence where else we decide to look for and potentially open a new location."

If you are in the ice cream business you might ask survey respondents what their favorite flavor or treat is. In addition, you might ask them if there are any other products they would like to see you sell. Examples might include smoothies, ice cream cakes, coffee, flavored iced teas, baked goods, sandwiches, etc. You might also probe whether they would be inclined to use a drive thru if one were provided.

Another question you might consider asking is which type of nearby businesses would prompt your visiting us more frequently? Examples might include cinemas, bookstores, restaurants, etc. Similarly, you might ask them to identify one or two businesses they would like to see become your next door neighbor(s). Furthermore, don't be shy about asking them to identify who they believe is your primary competitor.

If you want to learn more about **customer demographics** ask survey respondents to answer the following questions:

What is the highest level of **education** you achieved? (Answers might include a high school degree, some college, a college graduate, or a postgraduate degree).

What is the **occupation** of the head(s) of household? (Answers might include Professional, Manager, Sales, Business Owner, Educator, Retired, and Other).

If you are interested in learning about customer **psychographics** consider asking the following. Are you a homeowner? Do you listen to talk radio? Do you watch reality TV? Do you attend professional sporting events? Do you like jazz? What type of car do you drive? What is your favorite magazine? Do you own a laptop computer?

The information which is provided by customer surveys is valuable, especially when you consider that most of your competition is likely to know very little about who their customers are, what their demographic characteristics are, and what types of psychographics define their lifestyles.

I'm willing to bet that most small business owners will never invest in administering either a short form or long form customer survey. This doesn't mean that they can't be successful. However, it definitely decreases their chances for finding a "home run" location.

If you ever decide to open more locations or to grow your business through franchising you will learn that you will need to hire people—people who bring a lot of knowledge and experience to the table. Hopefully one of your hires will be a person who understands site selection and can help you pick winners and avoid losers.

With winners and losers in mind I would like to urge you to build your company around two towers of strength—operations and site selection. If you do this and you decide to become a franchisor, you will put yourself in the enviable position of potentially earning more than franchise fees, you will earn royalties. Royalties are where both your long term and big profits come from. They are what will allow you to live comfortably and enjoy the fruits of your success.

I hope that by reading this guidebook and by utilizing the information which it contains that you will enjoy lots of success in the near as well as long term future.

# CHAPTER TEN

# LOCATION, LOCATION, LOCATION

The most ubiquitous phrase in all of real estate is **Location, Location, Location.** In spite of most people's familiarity with this popular phrase many don't have a clear understanding of its true meaning.

If you conduct a Google search on **Location, Location, Location** you will find page after page of entries. Most of what you see or read is focused on residential real estate, especially single family homes. Very little mention is made of such commercial real estate stalwarts as retail and restaurants. After reading many pages of explanations, it became apparent to me that there is no common definition of this ages old axiom. Not only is this surprising, it's disappointing.

Whether your area of expertise is residential, industrial, office, retail, restaurant, or investment real estate, it is absolutely imperative that you understand the real meaning of **Location, Location, Location**. The same holds true if you are a business person or prospective business person, an appraiser, a lender, a city planner, a geographer, an economic development official, an executive with your local chamber of commerce, a property manager, a builder, a developer, or, a professor at the college level.

As a person with years and years of location experience, I am prepared to explain the real meaning of what is widely regarded to be the number one rule in real estate. When I think of the phrase **Location, Location, Location** I see a hierarchy of locations. To me, each of the three locations means something different. With that in mind, I want you to think of the geographic landscape being divided into three segments—large, mid size, and small.

While my goal is to describe **Location, Location, Location** from a retail and restaurant perspective, it behooves me to start off by providing you with a residential example. Why? Because what I'm about to describe is something I believe everyone can relate to. Assuming that you either own or have owned a single family home, I'm going to describe the three location factors which I'm confident led to your decision to buy.

No doubt the first thing you thought about was where (in which **area** or **community**) do I want to live? If you have children or have thought about starting a family, you most likely began your house search by looking at the quality of local schools. In addition, you probably looked at a number of other influential factors such as community size and character, walkability, proximity to major roads, shopping, and/or parks, and maybe even the extent of the street tree canopy. Doing this kind of time consuming homework helps explain what *Location Step #1* is all about.

Next, you probably drove through several **neighborhoods** as well as up and down countless streets—grid streets, curvilinear streets, no outlet streets, cul de sac streets, and boulevards—looking at a variety of houses while paying particular attention to those that were for sale. In doing so, you made a series of observations about curb appeal, the presence or absence of both sidewalks and street lights, street trees, landscaping, speed limits, etc. This combination of driving and scouting illustrates *Location Step #2*.

Lastly, more than likely, you visited each of the for sale **houses** which met your search criteria such as price, lot size, house size, kitchen size, number of bedrooms, number of bathrooms, garage size, and, the presence or absence of amenities such as a family room, basement, deck, patio, back yard, views, etc. Collectively, these attributes describe *Location Step #3*.

As a result of the aforementioned three step process, you used **Location, Location, Location** to guide your search efforts. Starting off by looking at a community (macro), then proceeding to looking at a particular neighborhood and/or one or more local streets, and ultimately to looking at one or more houses (micro), you demonstrated, knowingly or unknowingly, that there is no better way to achieve the American dream of home ownership than by relying on **Location, Location, Location**—the single best foundation for making "smart" location decisions.

With respect to retail and restaurants, I want you to picture a geographic **"area"** where a person or a company is interested in opening a business. This will require you to think at the macro scale. For example, think about a regional **"area"** or perhaps a downtown **"area."** These are destinations which are capable of attracting lots of people for lots of different reasons. Now, ask yourself why this particular **"area"** is an attractive location? Could it be because of the presence of one or more anchor stores, a large critical mass, an affluent surrounding population, a high traffic count, a significant number of retail stores, lots of restaurants, a large daytime population, or simply because it is located in the path of growth?

For most professionals and experienced business people, identifying this part of the location process is an essential first step in retail and restaurant site selection. As a result of having done their *homework*, they are capable of pinpointing a desirable **"area"**—in this case, a particular business corridor or street—fairly quickly and with relative ease. By performing this important exercise, you have taken *the first step* in the **Location, Location, Location** process.

Identifying *the second step* in **Location, Location, Location** is where the hard work really begins. Now you need to focus your attention on a specific **"site"**—something which is much more difficult for the untrained person to do. Here is where you need to determine if a particular retail or restaurant **"site"** meets the critical **PASTA V** test which was identified in Chapter One. Just in case you've forgotten, **"P"** stands for Parking, **"A"** for Access, **"S"** for Signing, **"T"** for traffic, **"A"** for Activity, and **"V"** for Visibility. Only if all of these attributes receive high marks will the **"site"** you are evaluating merit further consideration.

*The third step* in the **Location, Location, Location** process is not difficult to analyze but is often overlooked. It describes a specific **"space."** This is where you need to look both long and hard at the adequacy of critically important factors such as building setback, building frontage, building depth, window area, storefront signing, curb appeal, and, if you are in the restaurant business, an increasingly important amenity—outdoor seating. This is where you will need to determine whether or not a particular **"space"** receives a passing grade.

Because site selection is all about paying attention to details, I religiously rely on a **Site Selection Scorecard** like the one identified in Chapter Seven. This important tool keeps me not only organized but focused on the task at hand. It also allows me to make the best use of my time. Most importantly, it provides me with a **systematic** approach to making factual rather than emotional decisions.

Unlike buying a house, there is no room for emotion when it comes to making "smart" retail and restaurant location decisions—a lesson some people never learn. If their business fails, these people often blame failure not on the quality of food or merchandise or service, but on one factor—their location.

Retail and restaurant site selection pros know for a fact that "**area**," "**site**", and "**space**" play a primary role in the location decision-making process. Very importantly, they understand that the strength of their real estate strategies and the *homework* they complete can result in success.

Unfortunately, very few start-up businesses as well as some expanding businesses, including more than a few retail and restaurant franchises, don't have detailed or adequate site selection criteria, standards, and strategies to help guide their real estate decisions. Many of them stop doing their *homework* once they've identified a particular "**area**." They believe, incorrectly, that if they have identified the right "**area**" location that they can't go wrong and can justify making a major financial investment. Sadly, nothing could be further from the truth!

Other, wiser individuals, proceed to the second location step and are satisfied that they'll succeed for the simple reason that they've found the right "**site**." However, they may be in for a big surprise if they haven't completed their *homework*. For instance, a danger signal will occur when one or more of the variables comprising **PASTA V** is either missing or ranks poorly.

Steven Tanger, CEO of Greensboro, North Carolina based Tanger Factory Outlout Centers, Inc., sums up the key importance of "**site**" when he says: " . . . the best tenant mix is ultimately contingent upon the quality of the site." He continues by saying " . . . the quality of any development . . . is primarily contingent upon the quality of the site."

This is a good time to emphasize that the quality of a "**site**" has a lot to do with the future success of a retail or restaurant business. I think it is arguably the single most important component of the three location steps I've identified.

In the long run, it's the people who master not only "**area**" and "**site**" but the third and final location step who end up sleeping well at night. These are the people who do their *homework* (due diligence) in order to make sure they have the right "**space**." These are the individuals and companies who are the best equipped to see their respective businesses grow and prosper.

The most effective, but least common, way for you to find the right "**space**" is to become involved in the early planning stages of a new retail and/or restaurant development. Being engaged early in the process will provide you with the rare opportunity to not only educate a developer, but educate the people he or she works with, such as his or her project architect, about your requirements. Being a participant from the start will enable you, in many instances, to customize, to some degree, the space you decide to lease.

There is one other very important location component which needs to be mentioned. It has to do with the type of "**space**" a business ends up selecting. The three types of retail and restaurant "**space**," from the most to the least common as well as least to most expensive are: in line, end cap, and freestanding. In most instances, the type of "**space**" which is the best positioned to generate the highest sales volumes is freestanding. Next in order of sales productivity is end cap "**space**." In line "**space**" is typically the least productive type of retail or restaurant "**space**."

Among the reasons why freestanding "**space**," the type drug stores and many chain restaurants invest in prolifically, is the most desirable type of "**space**" is because such "**space**" is likely to (a) enjoy outstanding visibility, (b) benefit from having the ability to display more sign area, and (c) offers customers not only more parking but more convenient parking. Freestanding "**space**" which is located in the right "**area**" and on the right "**site**" can turn out to be a "home run" location, perhaps even a "grand slam" location. If you want a quick lesson in retail site selection, my advice is to pay particular attention to where chain drug stores have made location investments.

If you follow the evolution of drug store site selection, you will find that these businesses have a history of moving "up the ladder" from one type of location category to another. In other words, over a period of many years, they have graduated from in line to end cap to freestanding "**space**." In the process, they have been able to grow their sales.

Drug stores help illustrate why not all seemingly similar locations are created equal. The fact of the matter is that two similar drug store "**spaces**" located on two similar "**sites**" within the same general "**area**" can produce two different sales levels. Taking a page out of McDonald's site selection book, drug stores understand that the four corners of an intersection are, by no means, created equal. They know, depending on which "**site**" is selected, that there will be a variance in sales levels. What is the explanation for this? It starts with a comparison of **PASTA V** attributes followed by a determination of which store prototype (model) "**space**" is most capable of producing the highest sales and profits.

One other **Location, Location, Location** distinction you need to understand is that the meaning of this important phrase can change depending on whether it is daytime or nighttime. If, for instance, you are in the sub sandwich business, you need to be in an "**area**" with a strong daytime population in order to thrive. If the "**area**" you are considering doesn't have a large number of daytime employees you need to think long and hard about whether this is an "**area**" where you should make a major investment.

Conversely, if you are in the pizza business, you need to be in an "**area**" where a strong nighttime population exists—regardless of whether your business is dine in, caters to pick up/carry out customers, or delivers to surrounding households. If you choose an "**area**" without a lot of nearby rooftops you are making a decision which will, predictably, cost you dearly. Instead of remaining in business for a long time, you stand the risk of being what I commonly refer to as a "short timer."

The real learning curve in retail and restaurant site selection occurs when you have acquired a level of skills which enables you to consistently differentiate between location types. These location types consist of what I like to call "A+" (**Grand Slam**) locations, "A" (**Home Run**) locations, "B" (**Triple**) locations, "C" (**Double**) locations, and "D" (**Single**) locations.

From a frequency perspective, both "A+" and "A" locations are the most sought out, least common, and most expensive types of locations. Next in order of importance are "B" locations. On the other hand, both "C" and "D" locations—typically low rent locations which evidence a host of "**site**" and "**space**" related problems—are plentiful and, to use an old cliche, can be found "here, there, and everywhere."

My advice is never let cheap rent or bargain deals prompt your decision to either lease or acquire real estate. If you don't heed my advice you will not only be guilty of poor judgment, but of "rolling the dice." In site selection, minimizing risk and maximizing return on investment is "the name of the game."

Learning how to differentiate between two or more locations is not an easy task. By doing your *homework*, starting with data collection and extensive fieldwork, and by learning to be picky, you can eventually become a member of a relatively small group of people who have distinguished themselves by consistently making "smart" location decisions. In the process, you can take great pride and satisfaction in making the leap from being an amateur—someone who "thinks" a particular location is a good one, to being a pro—someone who "knows" that a particular location is, in fact, a good one, a winner!

I think this is a good time for me to share a very important thought with you regarding **Location, Location, Location**. It's something I've been thinking about more and more as I reflect not only on suburban development but the growing amount of redevelopment which is taking place within the beltway areas of our large cities. I'm talking about the impact transportation improvements have on **Location, Location, Location**. Whether changes are being made to accommodate the automobile or mass transportation, the bottom line is they can positively or negatively impact the quality of a location.

With regards to the automobile, a new highway interchange, a new road or street, the addition of a traffic signal, and/or the widening of a road or street will all have a *positive* impact on not only the "**area**" but the multiple "**sites**" along a corridor. Such improvements can provide greater convenience, and, over a period of time, (a) lead to new retail and restaurant development, (b) prompt other kinds of development and/or redevelopment such as an increase in both rooftops and daytime employment, and (c) increase the local tax base.

On the *negative* side, an overriding concern for safety can result in limiting curb cuts, requiring one way streets, adding medians, and reducing site access to right turns in and out. Whether individually or collectively, these types of changes can not only limit the desirability of a "**site**", but act as a deterrent to future development, negatively impact sales revenues, lead to short term as opposed to long term use, and adversely effect local property values.

The introduction of, as well as upgrades to, intra city rail and subway can also lead to changes in the attractiveness and desirability of both an "**area**" and a "**site**." Being at or near a transit stop can lead to all kinds of opportunities, including mixed use development. Here, you can expect to see the clustering of some or all of the following types of land uses: retail, restaurants, apartments, offices, residential condominiums, hotels, bars, cinemas, fitness facilities, and even sports complexes. I like to call the grouping of four or more synergistic uses a "game changer." Especially in core areas, these types of uses are capable of not only repopulating our cities but helping transform their urban fabric.

People who make site selection decisions understand that "time can change everything." With respect to the strength and viability of an "**area**," a "**site**," and/or a "**space**," the quality of a business location may fluctuate over time. In other words, over a short, intermediate, or long period of time, a particular location may transition from being outstanding, to being average or perhaps mediocre. What was once a "home run" location may, from time-to-time, be reduced to nothing more than a "double" or a "single" type of location.

In order to better understand this phenomenon, all you need to do is look at older commercial corridors. Whether they are a few blocks in length or extend mile after mile, with few exceptions, the dynamics of these once thriving business corridors will have changed over time. As a result, noticeable differences in the quality, vibrancy, and viability of a location may be more apparent.

People who make location decisions will remain amateurs if they pick the right "**area**" but the wrong "**site**" and/or the wrong "**space**." Likewise, they may not rise through the ranks if they select the right "**area**" and right "**site**" but end up selecting or developing the wrong "**space**." Picking the right "**area**," the right "**site**," and the right "**space**" is what, to cite another overused phrase, ends up "separating the men from the boys."

The next time you hear somebody talk about **Location, Location, Location**, ask him or her to explain its meaning. I can say, without any hesitation, that you won't always hear the same answer. Also, you're likely to find some people who will be honest and tell you that they have absolutely no clue what it means. But, by asking, there's a good chance you will learn something helpful.

Now that you have a better appreciation for, as well as much better understanding of the real meaning of **Location, Location, Location**, you are in the unique and enviable position of being able to separate yourself from the large number of people who think that picking a profitable retail or restaurant location is not that difficult. Some of these people include commercial realtors and developers who aren't knowledgeable about or experienced in site selection, franchisors and small businesses who don't employ any in-house real estate staff, and start-up businesses.

After a few years of making profitable retail and restaurant location decisions, your experience will eventually qualify you for membership in a small and select group, one where individuals take great pride in knowing that they are, in fact, members of an exclusive club. Given their expertise, some of these people are justified in thinking of themselves as "site selection snobs." Quite frankly, I think such a "credential" is something more real estate people and more business owners should aspire to. With that in mind, *I firmly believe the time has come for the real estate profession to create a new designation; the Certified Site Selection Specialist (CSSS).*

In the future, I hope you will share your new found wisdom about **Location, Location, Location** with your friends and business associates. In doing so, I hope you won't feel shy about reminding them that making the right location decision is like putting money *in* the bank. Conversely, choosing the wrong location is the equivalent of taking money *out* of their pocket—something they are likely to regret for a l-o-n-g, l-o-n-g time to come.

---

For those of you who are interested in learning about the origins of the phrase **Location, Location, Location,** I'm going to briefly cite an article written by columnist William Safire which appeared in the New York Times on June, 26, 2009.

The first written citation in which the popular phrase **Location, Location, Location** appeared was in 1956 in the Yale Book of Quotations. Its origins date to 1926 when a real estate classified ad appeared in the Chicago Tribune. It read: "Attention salesmen, sales managers: location, location, location, close to Rogers Park."

If you are unfamiliar with metropolitan Chicago, Rogers Park is a dense urban neighborhood which is located nine miles north of downtown Chicago. It borders Lake Michigan on the east and the city of Evanston on the north. Rogers Park is home to Loyola University. If you visit this area, you will find a mix of apartments, condominiums, and single family homes, as well as retail, bars, and restaurants.

---

In closing, here are some final thoughts regarding **Location, Location, Location.**

"Smart" location decisions are made with Location *Enhancement* and Location *Enrichment* in mind.

Remember, all locations are *not* created equal. Some will be more productive than others, meaning they will generate higher sales per square foot.

*McDonald's* and other successful restaurant and retail companies understand that site selection is not just about finding a site. It's about knowing what kind of sales a site can produce.

Christine Day, the former CEO of Vancouver, Canada based Lululemon, says " . . . the strength of our real estate strategy drives the strength of our business."

When considering which location to choose, *never focus on rent*. Always *focus on sales*.

Count on paying more for the best real estate. Neither "grand slam" nor "home run" locations come at bargain prices. In the long run, you get what you pay for.

# CONCLUSION

If you do your homework chances are very good that you will put yourself in a position to make "smart" location as well as "smart" site selection decisions. A very important part of doing your homework is reading, as opposed to skimming, through the pages of The ABC's of Site Selection.

Another part of doing your homework is getting organized. With this in mind, I would like to conclude my guidebook by providing you with a summary description of what I like to refer to as *The Ten Preliminary Steps to Site Selection Success.*

*Number One.* Have you taken the time to prepare a business plan? If the answer is no then you need to delay the start of your site search.

*Number Two.* Have you put together a list of site selection criteria? If not, you should determine which factors are the most important to the future success of your business concept. In other words, which factors are absolutely essential to being able to identify a "home run" location? This is a good time to revisit the Site Selection Scorecard information which is described in Chapter Seven.

*Number Three.* Have you determined who your primary customers are? Have you created a customer profile? If you are contemplating going the franchise route your franchisor should be a big help to you. If you have an existing business but haven't yet either conducted or analyzed any customer surveys then you need to do so as soon as possible. To have market intelligence information at your fingertips and not utilize it is inexcusable.

If you are a start-up business then you are at a bit of a disadvantage. However, knowing as much as possible about your competition and who their customers are can prove to be a good starting point.

*Number Four.* Have you decided where you will begin your site search? Will you be looking for a regional location or a community or neighborhood location? Will you be looking for a location with lots of nearby rooftops or one which is surrounded by a significant amount of daytime employees? Will you be looking for a location in a fast growth suburban area or will you concentrate your time and energies on finding a location in an older, underserved urban area?

*Number Five.* You need to think about how you are going to proceed. Will you go through the site selection search alone, or, will you do one or more of the following: work with a commercial realtor, knock on a prospective landlord's door, touch base with a property owner, or talk with a developer?

*Number Six.* Obtaining demographic information is important. What is even more important, however, is that you know what specific information to look for and analyze when you read thru a demographic report. Remember to focus on numbers as opposed to concentrating on percentages. If you need to, revisit and reread the contents of Chapter Eight.

Supplementing demographic information with psychographic information is recommended for business decision makers who already have one or more retail or restaurant locations. Here, your focus will be on understanding customer lifestyles; in other words, how people spend their money.

*Number Seven.* Once you have identified a particular location that you want to be in you need to conduct area research. It is critically important that you understand as much as possible about zoning, traffic counts, critical mass, anchors, competition, shadow businesses, subdivision activity, hours of operation, etc., etc.

*Number Eight.* At the same time you are conducting area research you should begin narrowing your list of site options. In determining which sites have the potential for becoming "home run" locations don't forget to revisit Chapter One—The Six Keys To Making "Smart" Site Selection Decisions. You will recall that this is where you were introduced to the very important PASTA V method of site analysis.

*Number Nine.* Once you have narrowed your list of candidate sites to one or two your next task will be to (a) begin estimating sales and (b) look at costs. It is very important that your emphasis be placed on future sales as opposed to costs. This, unfortunately, is where too many new or small businesspeople get it wrong. In addition, less seasoned site selection consultants are oftentimes guilty of making the same mistake by ignoring projected sales when completing their comparative site analyses. It is the hope of the author that neither you nor the resource person who is assisting you will make this all too common mistake.

*Number Ten.* If you have completed the many different types of homework which have been described in Steps 1-9 you will not only be well positioned to make a series of "smart" decisions, but, be able to negotiate either the purchase or the lease of prime real estate—the proverbial "home run" location. Once you have accomplished this important milestone you will be on the road to consistently being able to *pick winners and avoid losers.*

# ABOUT THE AUTHOR

Frank Raeon has been helping clients find high volume retail and restaurant locations for more than twenty five years. He has coined the term "home run" locations, a phrase you will see repeated many times during the course of reading The A B C's of Site Selection, as a way of describing such locations.

Within months of entering the real estate profession Frank began to observe that not all retail and restaurant locations are created equal. Understanding why one location was superior to another became his foremost goal and set him on the path to becoming a site selection specialist.

During his real estate career, Frank has focused his efforts primarily in the areas of site selection, tenant representation, and new development. Besides leasing and selling real estate he regularly advises the commercial development community on market opportunities, site planning, tenant mix strategies, building design enhancements, and zoning.

Working in the exciting field of site selection Frank has facilitated transactions which have culminated in the execution of numerous lease and purchase agreements. Examples of national, regional, and local market leading companies he has helped include Blockbuster, Buffalo Wild Wings, Dewey's Pizza, Donatos, First Watch, Graeter's Ice Cream, Izzy's, McDonald's, Pier 1 Imports, Servatii's, Subway, United Dairy Farmers, Walgreen's and Wendy's.

Primarily as a result of working with well respected national retail and restaurant companies Frank learned that that there is no substitute for doing homework—lots of it. By doing his homework Frank also learned that there is significantly more meaning to the phrase **Location Location Location** than meets the eye.

Frank is also the principal of *Location Decision Advisors*, a Cincinnati based real estate advisory company which helps both retail and restaurant companies better understand how to find "home run" locations. In addition to writing site selection success manuals, *LDA* provides demographics and psychographics assistance, designs, administers, and evaluates customer surveys, creates customer spotting maps, and, develops sales forecasts.

Frank's real estate background includes working as a Leasing and Sales Director for two Cincinnati area commercial developers. In the past he has taught continuing education classes on Site Selection for the Kentucky Real Estate Education Foundation as well as the Cincinnati and Dayton Area Boards of Realtors. Prior to becoming active in commercial real estate Frank worked as a City Planning and Development Director in Ohio and California. He is a charter member of the American Institute of Certified Planners (AICP).

Frank's undergraduate degree is from the University of Albany where he majored in both History and Geography. He earned his Master's degree in Urban Geography from the University of Cincinnati.

Frank is currently working on his second book: **Inside Site Selection.** It is based upon interviews with the people who are responsible for making retail and restaurant location decisions. It will detail the methodologies used by decision makers from throughout the United States in order to select "home run" locations.

Given his many years of experience and his ability to consistently produce "home run" locations Frank is fond of telling people that he will never waste their time. He relishes the opportunity to play a leadership role and considers himself to be a strategic partner in the site selection process—especially when assisting companies who, for one reason or another, do not employ the services of a person whose full time job responsibility is locating, negotiating, and securing prime real estate.

# Book Audience

The ABC's of Site Selection should have **broad appeal.** Its primary audience consists of small businessowners who are thinking about either future expansion or relocation, and people who want to start their own retail or restaurant business. You may be intrigued to learn that small businesses make up approximately 90% of all businesses in the United States as well as account for the majority of new jobs which are created.

Its secondary audience consists of realtors—primarily commercial realtors. As a group, commercial realtors are responsible for leasing as well as selling the vast majority of the retail and restaurant properties in the United States.

In addition, this book should have widespread appeal to new franchisees, small retail and restaurant franchise organizations which do not employ any dedicated real estate staff, and, developers of shopping center and mixed use properties.

Others who will find The ABC's of Site Selection instructive include directors of small business centers, SCORE counselors, Chamber of Commerce officials and their members, city planners, community and economic development officials, redevelopment corporations, and, college and university professors who teach courses in real estate, geography, urban planning, and business.

# INDEX

## A

access, 19, 35
activity, 20
adjacencies, 28
advertising, 79
airport locations, 60
ambiance, 79
amenities, 45
analog system, 79, 121
anchors, 28, 37, 83, 88, 107
areas of dominant influence, 80
awnings, 44, 70, 80

## B

basement locations, 45
bay windows, 64, 80
benchmarks, 80
board of advisors, 81
box signs, 25
brand equity, 81
brand recognition, 81
building setback, 29
building size, 80
building space
    parallel, 37, 99

perpendicular, 99
build to suit, 81

## C

camera, 82
cannibalization, 45
captive customers, 46
census tract, 82
Certified Site Selection Specialist
    (CSSS), 157
chambers of commerce, 82
city hall, 32, 68, 83
Claritas Inc., 38, 135, 139-40
color, 46-47
commercial realtors, 15, 47, 102, 113,
    132, 135-36, 165
common area, 47, 101
common area charges, 47-48
connectivity, 30
consultants, 47, 136
corridor dynamics, 83, 127
credit scores and financial statements, 84
curb appeal, 31, 128
curb cuts, 19, 35, 48, 51
customer
    address file, 84

collecting of information, 142
frequency, 84
lists, 85
occupations, 89
profile, 31, 141
relationships, 85
spotting maps, 86
target, 55
trip origin, 115
customer interviews, 55, 85
customer service, 51, 86, 106
customer surveys, 42, 56, 86, 143, 148, 164
exit, 121, 144
windshield, 58

**D**

daytime businesses, 87
daytime population, 32-33
decay curve, 48
demographics, 17, 29, 32, 135, 138, 141, 164
density, 33
destination-type business, 87
developers, 48, 165
drawing power, 88
drive times, 34
drop lane, 48

**E**

early-termination clause, 88
education levels, 48
ego, 89
emotion, 15, 54, 83, 89, 125, 132
entrepreneurs, 12
entryways, 31, 47, 49
exceptions and excuses, 90

**F**

facade enhancements, 49
fieldwork, 29, 32, 35
float, 90
focus groups, 90
freebies, 90
free rent, 49. *See also* freebies
frontage, 35

**G**

glass
  floor to ceiling, 90, 93
  high, 43-44, 92
goodwill, 91
grand opening, 91
gravity model, 91
ground lease, 91
growth indicators, 50
guidelines, 91-92
gut, 50, 54, 83

**H**

hierarchy of locations, 149
holdover clause, 92
hole in the fabric, 51
hours of operation, 29, 51

**I**

income levels, 51
infrastructure, 51
initial visit, 21

**K**

knee walls, 93

## L

landscaping, 93
land use, highest and best, 50
leakage, 93
lease agreement, 93
lighting, 51
location
  compatibility, 30
  definition, 35, 109
  distance, 115
Location Decision Advisors, 13, 47, 108, 164
locations
  college and university, 61
  community shopping center, 61
  convenience, 62
  convenience shopping center, 62
  corner lot, 62
  corner space, 63
  crossroads, 63
  dense urban and dense neighborhood, 63
  downtown, 64, 133
  egress, 49
  factory outlet, 65
  food cluster, 65
  food court, 66
  freestanding, 21, 24, 43, 62, 65-66, 68, 75, 123, 128, 153
  grand slam, 36, 129, 132, 153-54, 158
  highway interchange, 66, 68
  home run, 12, 15-16, 18, 36, 46, 50, 54, 58, 60, 75, 92, 108, 132, 135, 163-64
  icon, 67
  infill, 67-68
  intercept, 68
  interstate, 68
  lifestyle center, 69
  mixed land use, 70
  neighborhood, 71
  neighborhood shopping center, 71
  office building, 72
  office park, 72
  older business district, 72
  100%, 72
  outlot/pad, 72
  park and recreation, 73
  pedestrian friendly, 98
  power center, 74
  regional, 75, 160
  regional mall, 75
  street and sidewalk vendor, 75
  strip shopping center, 76, 99
  subway and train, 77
  tourist area, 77
  triple, 36, 132, 154
Location Step #1, 150
Location Step #2, 150
Location Step #3, 150

## M

market
  intelligence, 141, 143
  penetration, 95
  research, 36, 95, 136, 144
  share, 81, 95, 116
marketing, 94
McDonald's, 11, 95-96, 112, 163
median (barrier), 20, 36, 63, 95
median (demographic data), 95
memorable experience, creating a, 84
merchandising, 95
middle-turn lanes, 20
mom-and-pop businesses, 11, 45, 71, 78, 95
mystery shoppers, 95

## N

name recognition, 23, 58, 81, 91, 95-96

neighboring land uses, 52
neon signs, 24
newness, 96
niches, 96-97
nighttime businesses, 97
nighttime population, 36
numbers vs. percentages, 97

O

operations, 18, 97
origin of Location, Location, Location, 157
outdoor seating, 52, 59, 106
overage rent. *See* percentage rent

P

parking, 21
    customer, 22-23, 49, 53, 89
    employee, 22-23, 89
    garage and deck, 22
    garages, 53
    lots, 53
    metered, 22
    parallel or angled, 22
    ratio, 53
    shared, 108
    valet, 116
    visibility, 26
PASTA V, 27, 151-52, 154
patience, 98
peak periods, 98, 100
per capita income, 100
percentage rent, 99
personal observations, 52
photographs, aerial, 79, 132
pictures. *See* camera, 100
positive image, 51
primary trade area. *See* trade area
PRIZM, 38, 139-40
property maintenance, 101

proposal. *See* letter of intent
psychographics, 17, 38, 139, 148
psychological barriers, 29
public transportation, 102

Q

quantitative analyses, 102
questionnaires. *See* customer surveys

R

radius, 102, 115
real estate agent, 102
realtor. *See* commercial realtors
recessed entryways, 103
rent, 48
return on investment, 103
right turns, 20
rooftops, 36, 59
royalty fees, 104

S

safety, 22, 38
sale leasebacks, 104
sales
    correlated factors, 122
    estimates/forecasts, 38
    per capita, 104
    per parking space, 104
    per seat, 104
    per square foot, 104
sales transfer. *See* cannibalization, 54
SBA (Small Business Administration),
    105, 110
SCORE (Service Core of Retired
    Executives), 82, 105
seating, 105
sensory appeal, 106
service. *See* customer service, 86, 106

service drives, 107
service retailers, 107
shadow businesses, 107
sidewalks, 47, 54, 64, 73, 150
signing, 23, 59
site
  analysis/evaluation, 39, 83
  data collection, 32
  definition, 109
  desirability of, 87
  distance, 39
  grade, 26, 40, 54
  model, 54
  plan, 108
site searches
  daytime visits, 87
  nighttime visits, 97
  talking with nearby businesspeople, 43
site selection
  coach, 108
  criteria, 109
  growth, 112
  guidelines and standards, 40, 54, 91,
    109
  scorecard, 17, 54, 125, 129, 138, 143,
    151
  specialist, 82
slope. *See* site: grade
space
  depth, 33
  plan, 111
  previously occupied, 100
  second floor, 106
  size, 80, 111
  south- and west-facing, 110
  surplus, 113
  vanilla box, 116
speed limit, 40, 130
Starbucks, 84, 96
storefronts, 45, 76, 93, 112
street

going home side of the, 35
going to work side of the, 35
street furniture, 112
streets
  arterial, 45-46
  collector, 46
  grid, 50, 150
  primary, 45, 54
  secondary, 106
strip locations, 76
subjectivity, 113
surrounding business district, size of, 31
synergy, 41, 62, 66-67, 69, 71, 75, 88,
    123, 130-31
system for success, 55

**T**

TEAM (together everybody achieves
    more) mentality, 113
tenant improvement allowance, 114
tenant mix, 46, 56, 75, 95
trade area, 41
traffic, 25
  congestion, 42, 47, 54, 56-57, 62, 127,
    130
  count, 56
  generators, 56
  quality, 42
  signalization, 42
  stacking, 20, 42, 57, 62-63, 100
traffic lanes, number of, 52
transportation improvements, 155
trees, 26, 57, 93, 107, 115
triple net rents, 115
turning radius, 115

**V**

view corridors, 57
view time, 57

visibility, 25
voids analysis, 58

# W

walkways, covered, 83
window, pickup, 37
windows, 43, 110
women, 32, 38, 52, 117

# Y

Yellow Pages, 117

# Z

zip codes, 58
zoning, 23, 57, 59, 116, 163

LDA: HELPING YOU FIND HOME RUN BUSINESS LOCATIONS

HOME RUN

© COPYRIGHT 2010 L. Gray Huebls

**LDA: LOCATION DECISION ADVISORS**

Edwards Brothers Malloy
Oxnard, CA  USA
June 10, 2014